"This book is a poignant expression of how to break out of the survival mindset—and use our hardships to heal and grow."

—Kim Beckham, pastor and author of *Letters to the Heart*

"Every now and then, a book comes out and impacts our life. *Surviving or Thriving?* is that book that will give you insights into your actions and choices. A home run, Stepp!"

—Skip Miller, author of *ProActive Sales Management*

"The ability to attain success is often dictated by our own self-perception. Stepp's book is a guide to help you achieve your own personal and professional goals by focusing on the facts and giving you the tools to attain positive and prosperous results."

—Allen Roberts, VP, Cox Business Services

"This inspiring book helps us identify behaviors which signal we have grown satisfied with merely hanging on; and introduces behaviors which shift our mindset from victims to victors."

—Ann Lott, CEO, Dallas Housing Authority

SURVIVE OR THRIVE?

Always Thrive —

Lloyd Sp[...]

Paula,
Choose to thrive...
Bless your life.
Suzi Streit

SURVIVE OR THRIVE?

Creating THE LIFE YOU WANT Out of THE LIFE YOU HAVE

Stepp Stevens Sydnor
with Suzi Streit

iUniverse, Inc.
New York Bloomington Shanghai

SURVIVE OR THRIVE?
Creating THE LIFE YOU WANT Out of THE LIFE YOU HAVE

iUniverse books may be ordered through booksellers or by contacting:

iUniverse
1663 Liberty Drive
Bloomington, IN 47403
www.iuniverse.com
1-800-Authors (1-800-288-4677)

Because of the dynamic nature of the Internet, any Web addresses or links contained in this book may have changed since publication and may no longer be valid.

The views expressed in this work are solely those of the author and do not necessarily reflect the views of the publisher, and the publisher hereby disclaims any responsibility for them.

All scripture quotations, unless otherwise indicated, are taken from the HOLY BIBLE, NEW INTERNATIONAL VERSION ®. NIV ®. Copyright © 1973, 1978, 1984 by International Bible Society. Used by permission of Zondervan Publishing House. All rights reserved.

Scripture quotations marked KJV are taken from the 21st Century King James Version ®, copyright © 1994. Used by permission of Deuel Enterprises, Inc., Gary, SD 57237. All rights reserved.

ISBN: 978-0-595-42294-4 (pbk)
ISBN: 978-0-595-86631-1 (ebk)

Printed in the United States of America

This book is dedicated to my kids: Nick, Nicole, and Josh Sydnor

Contents

Acknowledgments

I want to express my heartfelt gratitude to all those in my life who have helped me see with greater clarity the difference between surviving and thriving. To pastor Kim Beckham, who sparked the fire for this subject. To Suzi Streit, my business associate and good friend, whose ideas, editing, and encouragement helped shape this book. To Sue Carrington of Carrington Communications, my communications consultant and writer, who has helped to give wings to my thoughts. To Mary Ann Lackland of The Fluency Organization, Inc., for consultation and direction. To Karen Dodd, for her devotion to our work, the long hours editing and for her eagle eye, constant attention to details, and encouraging smile. To my children, Nick Sydnor, Nicole Sydnor, and Joshua Sydnor: you are the very reason to thrive. And to my mom, Sidney, who is my greatest fan and constant encourager. To my best friend and brother, Rick Sydnor, for calling me almost every day just to say hello.

Other friends and family who saw me through the storms of life are Richard Spencer, Jim Little, Robert Norton, and Newt Farrar. Thanks also to Debbie Weicht, Donna Wesson, Dianne Davis, Mario Zandstra, and Bobbie Woods. I am blessed with wonderful friends, family, and colleagues—and an amazing abundance of love.

Preface

On the hit television show *Survivor*, contestants try to outwit, outplay, and outlast everyone else until they're the sole survivor. Songs like Elvis Presley's "Only the Strong Survive" and Gloria Gaynor's "I Will Survive" are deeply embedded in our popular culture. Survival seems to be a recurring theme in today's popular culture. This pervasive theme of survival extends to real life as well. We survive natural disasters as well as everyday events. Surviving has been elevated to an art form!

It's no wonder, then, that we think just getting through each day is enough to ask for in life. We tend to stop at survival instead of taking the next step toward a new and more fulfilling existence. If we've faced trauma and tragedy, we may stay linked to our troubles, insisting we're still fighting for our life, long after the actual threat has passed. We may have a habit of holding onto our survival mentality, rather than using our hardships to heal and grow and to help others learn from the lessons of our own experience.

This book is about moving from a surviving mindset to a thriving one. It's about doing more than just surviving in this life and instead rethinking your situation so that you can create a better life. It's based on my own life trials and what I've learned from others in my work as a leadership and sales trainer and motivational speaker. I have also added stories of others who have persevered and overcome challenging events. Over and over, I've found that the troubles of our lives, as much as they pummel us, are often treasures in the making—if we can transcend our pain to see things differently. But how do we change how we see?

For me, it started with a dark event: an unexpected divorce. In the depths of my pain and the process of the event, I was visited one day by Kim, a pastor and a good friend. While shoring up my spirits, Kim mentioned that many people were observing how I responded to my situation. Because I speak often on self-improvement topics, they were watching to see if I walked the walk or just talked the talk. He said I couldn't just survive; I needed to do more.

Long after Kim left, what he said about "more than just surviving" stayed with me. Later that same week, my oldest son came by to see how I was doing. My situation, he said, seemed a lot like Job's, the biblical character who lost all that he had—family, fortune, and health—but never lost his faith. Because of his unwavering spirit, Job was eventually restored to a new and better life. I felt encouraged by my son, who in his own way was telling me to go beyond surviving. However, could I survive as Job did and actually thrive again?

The next morning, deep in thought over a cup of coffee, I wrote down the behaviors I saw in myself as I struggled to recover from the blows of my current situation. I had many conflicting feelings and was also unsure about whether I was going to make it through the day. My bills tripled due to court costs while my ability to work diminished each day. I felt the darkness of depression closing in on me. What I needed to do was to get back on my feet. However, my foundation was shifting and unsure. I was trying to remain balanced and upright, while the ground underneath was in constant change. I realized that by not taking positive steps, I had become just a Survivor. What I needed to do was to think differently, turn myself around, and become a Thriver. Armed with these thoughts, I began to write down in one column what surviving looked like. Then I wrote in another column what thriving would look like. I began with the simple question, "If I was just trying to survive this situation, what would I be doing, acting, saying, and thinking? If

I moved beyond surviving to a more thriving life, what would I be doing, acting, saying, thinking?" Soon I had a very good outline that helped me begin the process of navigating through my current problems and getting my life back on course. I asked my friend and co-worker, Suzi Streit, to help me categorize these Survivor/Thriver behaviors and further define them in action. Suzi, too, was in survival mode as she worked to save her own marriage.

As we shared our stories with each other, we came up with ideas on how to get past the pain and start rebuilding our lives. From that, we created our first *Survive or Thrive?* seminar. Today we are using these ideas to help people through many struggles and trials in life other than divorce. Our seminars cover handling change, becoming a better communicator, understanding your hidden talents, and becoming goal oriented, as well as coaching individuals and executives toward professional and personal improvements.

Right now, you may be struggling to survive a bitter blow—a failed relationship or business, or perhaps the death of a dream or of a loved one. You may be swept away in the emotions that the hardships of life can carry, from shock to fear, from loneliness to desperation. You could be a teenager who didn't get a full scholarship and is giving up the dream of a professional career, or you could be a recently single mom or dad wondering how you are going to make it. If you are going through a difficult time and are unsure of your future, know that you're in good company: the company of every person on Earth! Everyone, at some time in their life, will be faced with difficulties. Just as we can count on the sun to come up and go down today, we can count on life's difficulties and unexpected changes to visit us. Like a hurricane, it sweeps in without an invitation—ripping open our dreams, crushing our future, and leveling our spirits—if we let it. The question is, will you let it? Will you let adversity keep you from your dreams?

Chapter One

No One Said Life Is Fair

From a tsunami in Thailand to Hurricane Katrina, from bombings in Iraq to an avalanche in the Himalayas, stories of miraculous survival seem to occur in every corner of our world.

For most of us, being rescued from swelling flood waters or from the icy slopes of Mt. Everest will not be something that we will experience in our lifetimes. Still, life is fickle, leaving us with surging or unscalable situations.

> **"When it's dark enough, you can see the stars."**
> *Ralph Waldo Emerson*

During a break at one of my company's seminars, a woman asked me, "Do you think life is fair?"

I was quick to answer, "No, it's certainly not."

To my surprise, she said, "I think it is. Sooner or later, it breaks everybody's heart."

Later on that evening, I thought about what she had said and concluded that, in a way, she was right. At some time, before our individual lives end, we will have our hearts broken. I know I have had my share of disappointments and surprises. Parents who divorced when I was five. A father who was married and divorced seven times. Girls I fell in love with, but they didn't feel the same about me. Romances that seemed promising but didn't work out. Dreams that I was sure would work but ended up failing. Jobs that didn't work out, leaving me in financial turmoil. Two marriages that didn't work out. Accidents and endless changes in the economy and weather all seem to continue to arrive daily on my door step.

In some ways, I guess life is fair because everyone will experience a level of hardship sometime. We are all in the same boat when it comes to life challenges. I once heard that life is like a deck of cards: you have to play the hand you are given. Meaning, I need to make a great life out of the hand dealt to me. Some children, like me for example, are born and raised in a multiple-divorce family that lives from paycheck to paycheck. Others are born into a financially secure family where commitment is valued. Still, hardships will be common to both. I remember one hardship in my life with vivid clarity.

Receiving Bad News

I was just getting out of my car in the parking lot next to the high school sports stadium when a stranger came up and asked me my name. After I gave him my name, he gave me a legal divorce notice. I stood there feeling confused, humiliated, and embarrassed. People were walking by; some were watching the look on my face. My emotions were as strong as a hurricane. That moment felt like Katrina's aftermath—the treasures of a lifetime destroyed in an instant.

Sitting in the stadium seats, I remember I felt disoriented and confused. I was trying to read through the legal papers but not understanding the strong legal language. I was angry and hurt at the same time. I felt everyone in the stadium knew about my situation. All eyes were on me and every conversation from the people around me seemed to be about me. I felt almost paranoid and lost. I wanted to crawl under a rock and hide. Later my son, who played on the high school soccer team, needed to see me about getting some money for the concession stand. I knew he didn't know about the oncoming divorce, and I felt the heaviness of the situation weighing in on me. My chest felt tight and I couldn't breathe, much less pay attention to the game.

During our twenty-year marriage, my wife and I had had our ups and downs, but I never thought that it would come to this. This was my second marriage, and I didn't want another divorce. Currently we were experiencing some difficult challenges in our relationship, but the legal papers came as a shock.

At that point in time, we had recently bought our six-acre dream home, the bills were getting paid, we had many friends, and our connection to our church and community was a source of great joy. The kids were engaged in school activities, and they were at that age where we didn't need a babysitter. In ten more years, we would have an empty nest. I had been looking forward to those years.

How Did This Happen?

About three years prior to the divorce, I got laid off from a job that I was sure would be a lifetime career. I had been helping other business owners and CEOs grow their business. So, I decided to begin a new business in the same field.

I began my new business by meeting with executives I knew and felt needed what I had to offer. Soon I added one employee and then another. After a year, we needed to expand out of a small room in our home into more office space. We kicked around the idea of adding a portable building to our current home but decided that a bigger home with an office in the back of the house would be just perfect. I had always dreamed of waking up and stepping into a home office. Imagine no traffic or long drives to navigate!

After some house hunting, we discovered a wonderful deal. It was a large home on six acres that just needed some TLC (which included paint—something I hate to do). The property was our dream home and had a separate three-car garage which we remodeled into an office three months after we purchased the home. Our business was getting off the ground. I had hired another speaker to help with the seminars as well as an office manager and two new sales people. Life was good and business was growing.

Of course, the challenges of creating a new company brought certain frustrations into the marriage. The business income was growing but unpredictable at times. Business deals I proposed and was sure to win, we lost. Marketing and selling our services was up to me. My sales people were new and needed training. Speakers needed to be trained on out-of-town trips, which created tension, suspicion, and conflict at home. We had a lot of plates to spin with three kids, sports, church, and extended family commitments. However, with determination and zeal, our future looked good. I was in my mid-forties and I pictured life at this time like having a fun picnic by a gentle calm lake. It was a great life, not a perfect life, and I was enjoying the journey. All was quiet until the storm rolled in.

Things Suddenly Change

Living in East Texas has lots of advantages, especially if you enjoy camping. There are many clear beautiful lakes, huge towering pine trees and gentle hills, as well as an endless supply of small towns and farm roads to discover. I love camping with my kids. I remember one camping trip we were in nylon tents and sleeping bags at Hawkins Park in East Texas. The weather was a typical June summer day—sunny and hot with a cloudless blue sky. During the evening, however, the wind picked up, the clouds moved in, and the lighting started dancing between the tall pine trees. I remember the storm came so fast we barely had time to run to our car while dodging lightning bolts and hoping one of those large pine trees didn't fall on us.

I was so scared, but I was "Dad"—the strong man running to the car with kids in tow, just knowing I was going to get crushed by a pine tree or fried by a lightning bolt. I gave up the idea of camping, left the rain-soaked tents and sleeping bags, and headed home. On the way back, I couldn't help thinking how unwise it was to go camping that day, but the weather report had said sunny and clear.

I realize now how that analogy described my life at the time. Everything *seemed* sunny and clear. However, storms in life come quickly and unexpectedly. Just when I was enjoying a fun picnic by the lake, a boulder crashed into my beautiful world, sending waves of despair and confusion in every direction.

Storms affect everyone. Amid the divorce, my children were very confused. In-laws and parents were desperately trying to make sense of it all. Some friends took sides while others remained neutral. Rumors spread and false stories tumbled around us like an avalanche, leaving me depressed. It became almost impossible to keep focused and productive at work. I would sit for hours in my office in a comatose state. The phone would ring, and I didn't hear it. I would go teach a seminar and not remember where I was, how I got there, or what I said. Have you ever been so afraid or distraught you couldn't move or think? That's how it was for me.

Each day brought a new emotional ripple. Anger. Shame. Blame. Defeat. The court dates were a sounding board for the attorneys to bring up new hurtful accusations to make me look like I was an unfit parent and harmful to my children. Humiliation, embarrassment, fear, rejection, and loneliness became my new unwanted friends.

Mostly, I was scared, barraged by continuous self-questioning and doubt. Questions like: How will this impact my kids' future and their hopes for a strong marriage? How did this happen so fast? What do people think of me? Will my pain ever end? What will happen to my business? How am I going to get the strength to get through lunch?

I had worked for twenty years to create a world that was part of the life, liberty, and pursuit of happiness known as the American dream. Didn't I deserve it? Gone was the world we had worked so hard to build. I now had to move out of our dream home. And for the next nine months, my new home would be a small camper in a trailer park. An overnight downsize from 4000 square feet to 250 square feet. I felt like the world had just dealt me a hand that I never wanted.

We just assume that our neighbors have the "good life" and problem-free, happy homes. However, the truth is that all of us will face adversity. Some are at the front of the storm, not knowing they are in its path; others are in the middle of a life crisis. Still, others are taking inventory of the storm after it has passed. No one said that life is fair except in one sense: life is unfair for everyone.

No Permission Asked

Funny thing about change. Whether it's good or bad, it doesn't ask for permission to show up. Just open the paper or watch any newscast and you will see someone winning the lottery alongside someone losing a child to a horrible tragedy. Someone finds the love of their life, while someone else has a broken heart due to a failed relationship. Change happens, and it doesn't ask for your permission.

Sometimes hardships arrive in waves. Sometimes they are big problems, and sometimes they are small and accumulate quickly. I remember a time when a friend had taken over the payments on my car with the expectation that once the note was paid I would sign over the title to him. Now—surprise!—my friend decided he didn't want the car anymore, broke his agreement, and dropped the car off at my office. As I was driving home in a car that I couldn't afford and needed desperately to sell, a rock bounced off a construction truck and hit my windshield leaving a huge crack. Minutes later while filling up the empty tank with gas, I noticed the driver's rear tire was flat. I found an air compressor and scrounged around for fifty cents in the bottom of my computer bag. When I deposited my money, it didn't work. And I didn't have another fifty cents. So, I decided to change the tire. However, when I checked the spare tire, it was flat, too. All these irritating problems in the midst of bigger problems surfaced in a matter of a few hours. It seems like a little irritation now, but at the moment it was a small storm to me. Could life get any more challenging at this point? Challenges come in waves.

I had been through challenges before. I recall another situation that happened just before I started my own consulting firm. A former boss started a company not too far from where I lived. His company was a new start-up, only two years old. We had become reacquainted while I was doing a contract job for another company. My old boss's company had a service we could use for the contact customer.

In the process of getting the two companies working together on the project, I was offered a full-time job with both companies. Both had good offers on the table for employment. However, I felt more loyalty to my old boss since we had a long history. He needed my expertise and assistance, and I was glad to help. I felt it was a wise and good move—and a company that I could stay with until retirement. I ran my decision by others just to make sure I was making a wise move. I had looked at the company and its current challenges, asked a lot of questions, and felt I understood the present challenges. I accepted the position with the hope of having a long, profitable future with them.

Then, a change occurred. After just three months, the company's investors pulled their support. I was faced with being laid off along with over two hundred other people. To make things worse, I was laid off at the end of November, with Christmas just around the corner. My loyalties to my old boss resulted in no severance pay and travel expenses that were unlikely to be reimbursed.

My financial situation was desperate. Christmas was twenty-five days away. I had enough financial resources to cover the first-of-the-month bills and get us through December 15. I was angry and felt stupid and used. How could this happen, and why at this time? Telling my fellow employees that everything would be OK felt good at the office water cooler, but when we parted, I was still left with the harsh realities that in fifteen days there would be no money.

That night I remember lying in bed, paralyzed by fear. One part of me said, "You can't get another job in two weeks; it will take too long. You will never, ever make it. What a loser you are." I told myself, "You did all the right things, looked at the company, asked the right questions, and sought wise counsel. And look how things turned out. God, you must hate me. Well, I hate you too."

At the same time, another part of me was thinking, "What did I learn from this? I have gotten out of tight places before. I can do it again. I do have options, my life isn't over, and I am a winner, not a loser. God, thanks for helping me out!" I found that thinking this way helped me feel less depressed and more hopeful.

Change happens, and even the innocent get hurt. That night, I decided on a course that turned out better than I could have expected. In fact, what happened beginning that night was an incredible turnaround for me that I will share with you later on in this book. I learned key principles from this experience that, looking back, I could not have learned any other way (see Chapter 5, *Victim Versus Warrior*).

I discovered that even though I had been blindsided by change, I still had choices. I could run and hide, or I could march boldly onward with a solid plan to turn the tide.

Turning the Tide

The movie *Castaway* is one of my favorites because of its powerful message. In it, a FedEx worker (played by Tom Hanks) survives a plane crash and is stranded for several years on a tropical island. After being rescued, he is asked how he managed to keep going, day after day, with his sanity intact. Hanks' character replies, "I never knew what the tide would bring in."

What a powerful thought! Whenever I'm facing life's challenges, I think about what the tide may bring in. On a good day, it may bring an unexpected gift. For the *Castaway* character, his gift was a Porta-Potty, which he used to create a sail; attached to a raft, the sail allowed him to get off the island. A portable toilet—what an unexpected gift!

In moving through my layoff crisis, the unexpected gift was the birth of a new business—one that embodies many of the principles I've found helpful in my own turnaround. I named the company TurnAround Training Solutions. My company's focus is helping organizations and individuals transform from a surviving mindset to a thriving one—like the *Castaway* character who maintains his hope expecting the tide to bring in something good. Were it not for my being toppled from what I thought was a secure situation, I would not have found my life's true calling. I didn't know I could write seminars and do them for a living. What seemed to be a tragedy actually became a gift.

I had no control over the change that swept through my life. However, I did have a choice about how I responded to it. Regardless of the agony of my situation—in the layoff and then in the divorce—I realized I was still responsible for creating my future. I once heard that ten percent of life is what happens to you, and ninety percent is how you respond. What happens *to* us is not nearly as important as what emanates *from* us. As it was for me with the birth of TurnAround Solutions, change can be the seed for new growth and a whole new way of seeing and being.

> **"A certain amount of opposition is of great help to a man. Kites rise against, not with, the wind."**
> *John Neal*

How much of our lives do we lose when challenges hit and we focus all our energy on just trying to survive? We miss out on the unexpected gifts. The good news is we can do much more than survive.

How about you? Where are you stuck? Are you looking for an unexpected gift? Don't overlook the little things—the small opportunities that you could miss because your mind is focused on just surviving.

Think about what you have been through or what you're going through and ask yourself this question. Will you just survive ... or thrive?

Insight

A Perfect Picture of Peace[1]

Long ago a man sought the perfect picture of peace. Not finding one that satisfied, he announced a contest to produce this masterpiece. The challenge stirred the imagination of artists everywhere, and paintings arrived from far and wide. Finally the great day of revelation arrived.

The judges uncovered one peaceful scene after another, while viewers clapped and cheered.

The tensions grew. Only two pictures remained veiled. As a judge pulled the cover from one, a hush fell over the crowd. A mirror-smooth lake reflected lacy, green birches under the soft blush of the evening sky. Along the grassy shore, a flock of sheep grazed undisturbed. Surely this was the winner.

The man with the vision uncovered the second painting himself, and the crowd gasped in surprise. Could this be peace? A tumultuous waterfall cascaded down a rocky precipice; the crowd could almost feel its cold, penetrating spray. Stormy-grey clouds threatened to explode with lightning, wind and rain. In the midst of the thundering noises and bitter chill, a spindly tree clung to the rocks at the edge of the falls. One of its branches reached out in front of the torrential waters as if foolishly seeking to experience its full power.

A little bird had built a nest in the elbow of that branch. Content and undisturbed in her stormy surroundings, she rested on her eggs. With her eyes closed and her wings ready to cover her little ones, she manifested peace that transcends all earthly turmoil.

Chapter Two

Learning to Manage Our Self-Talk

Mark sits alone at a bar. He has closed the doors on his business, a business that was successful beyond his dreams for over a decade. However, the economy has taken a turn for the worse, and Mark's company couldn't weather the storm.

The failure of his business is taking a toll on his marriage. Mark's wife says she is tired of living like this. She is frustrated and doesn't understand how they came to lose the business; she wasn't involved in the day-to-day business events. Because Mark has a master's degree in business, she wonders how this could have happened. Their relationship is awkward and distant.

The banks and vendors are calling daily to get some answers—and to get their money. Mark looks into the mirror and sees a defeated man unable to provide for his family. He voluntarily took his BMW back to the bank because he didn't want the neighbors to see the repossession truck at his house. Mark is understandably embarrassed, humiliated, and suffering from the loss.

Mark's self-confidence has plummeted, and he questions his future. Mark feels depressed and unable to function—in short, a failure. He is sure that his family, friends, and co-workers see him as a failure and a loser, too. Mark is questioning his religious training and faith. He is now in a bar, hoping that the alcohol will deaden the pain. Just getting through the day is painful. Mark is in survival mode, and this is where he will stay until he sees that his negative self-talk is beating him down.

Is Mark creating a fictional world that will soon become his real one? How does his "I'm a failure and a loser" motto keep him feeling sad and depressed? His story is based on little fact; yet he is behaving as if it were a true story. He is guessing what his family, friends, and co-workers think. But does he really know? Where do these thoughts come from? They come from our self-talk. "Self-talk" is a term for the internal dialogue we rehearse regarding what we believe about ourselves. The way we think about ourselves is powerful and has a direct result on the way we live. In Mark's case, his self-talk is sending him into a deep depression with feelings of inadequacy. If Mark continues with this type of self-talk, he will soon create exactly what he is thinking. In the end, he will create a self-fulfilling prophecy.

Mark is stuck trying to survive the closing of his business. Mark's identity is wrapped up in the success of his business, too. This happens to a lot of people. When their plans succeed and things are going well, they get a certain level of praise and honor from friends and family. However, when circumstances change for the worse, they tend to lose their way.

For most people, their jobs and titles provide them with identity. When the job is lost, they lose some of their identity. To survive a job loss, people need to manage the stories that come from their self-talk. For Mark to move through this survival-thinking toward thriving-thinking, he must first manage his self-talk. What Mark tells himself determines what he feels, how he acts, and who he will eventually become.

Self-talk is very powerful, so understanding how we can manage it helps us control our feelings, attitudes, and actions. Our self-talk can be negative, positive, or neutral. In Mark's case, his self-talk starts with his understanding of facts versus stories.

So, how does Mark's negative self-talk keep him from moving on? Let's look at the facts of Mark's story and then look at his thoughts. What do we know about Mark that we could say is true? What are the facts? We know that Mark had a business that lasted a decade and that Mark closed his business due to a downward turn in the economy. We know that he is married, has kids, and has a master's degree in business. The bank and vendors are calling Mark. He had a BMW that went back to the bank. These are the things that we know to be true because we can verify the facts.

So, what is Mark's negative self-talk?

Mark is thinking, "I lost my business, so I am a loser and a failure. My wife wants to leave me and thinks I am a loser."

Mark's negative self-talk is creating a fictional story. The question that needs to be answered is whether or not Mark is a "loser."

Let's take a closer look. Mark is a self-starter, has incredible ambition and drive, and has critical-thinking and problem-solving skills. He can negotiate conflict well and can manage relationships between family, employees, and vendors. He can plan and execute a strategy, stay on task, and complete and bring closure to a plan. He can balance work and family and somehow still find time to volunteer for good causes. He can also sell products, prospect for new customers, train employees, handle advertising, and navigate complicated conversations with his CPAs, attorneys, and banks.

Does this sound like a loser to you?

Mark needs to change his negative self-talk to positive self-talk. His facts are true, but the story he creates from the facts are causing him to slip into the darkness of depression. Mark should grieve the loss of his business; this is a normal process in the survival mode.

However, Mark can create a different outcome by examining the facts and managing his self-talk and story.

> **"The trick is in what one emphasizes.**
> **We either make ourselves miserable, or we make**
> **ourselves happy. The amount of work is the same."**
> *Carlos Castaneda*

Here's another example. One day I had a conversation with my oldest son, who was home from college for the summer. We discussed his need to find a job. He agreed and a few days later reported that he had stopped at several companies to fill out a job application. A few weeks later I noticed that he still didn't have a job. I was getting upset at his lack of motivation. So I asked him how the job hunting was coming. He said he hadn't done anything since filling out the applications. Immediately I started creating negative stories. I found myself getting upset and angry. My thoughts were critical:

"He's going to turn out to be a lazy bum."
"He thinks gas money grows on trees."
"He is so irresponsible and immature."

These thoughts are just stories created from my opinion of the facts. The things I was telling myself about my son and his situation were not very flattering, nor were they based on the person I know him to be. My self-talk was immediately negative and created a fictional story that got me all worked up.

So what were the facts in this example?

- He needed to get a summer job.
- He needed extra money.

- He did go to several companies and fill out applications.
- He did speak to several managers and ask them questions.

The cure for my negative self-talk was to neutralize the fictional story I'd created by looking at the facts again and getting more information from my son.

With an open and relaxed body language and tone, I talked to my son about the situation. Starting with the facts, I said, "Son, a few weeks ago we agreed you needed to find a job. You need gas money. You said you went to several companies, filled out applications, and spoke to several managers. [These are the facts.] I am thinking that you don't really want a job and that you are assuming I am going to give you gas money. [This is my story.] Is this true?"

My son answered. "Dad, I'm honestly not sure what to do next. I walked in off the street, talked to the manager, and filled out an application. They said they would call, but they haven't. [These are the facts.] Maybe they don't like me or want me there. [This is his story.] I don't know what to do next."

I could tell by the way he spoke that his confidence was very low. No one had called back after the initial interviews. My son was focusing on his own negative self-talk.

I looked at him and asked him if he felt stuck. He said yes. He wanted a job but didn't know what to do next. Then we spent the next hour talking about interview strategies. The conversation was open, honest, and fun. The next day my son was working on a new plan and felt much better. His confidence increased. Eventually he got a great job.

Consider what my attitude and tone would have been if I had acted on my negative self-talk story before I looked at the facts. I would have wasted my time with him, fuming over his laziness. Then I would have taken my emotional shotgun and blasted him with hurtful words. A father-son war would have been just around the corner. Imagine what impact this incident could have had on our long-term relationship if I hadn't stopped to separate the facts from my own fictitious story.

> **"Our real blessings often appear to us in the shape of pains, losses, and disappointments."**
> *Joseph Addison*

Stinking Thinking

All of us suffer from "stinking thinking," another term for negative self-talk. I once heard sales guru Zig Ziglar at a seminar. He said something that I would never forget. He said that you have to do a check-up from the neck up, because it's all happening between your ears. Psychologists tell us that we act based on what we're feeling. If you feel sad, you act sad. But where does the sadness come from? What we feel will be determined by what we're telling ourselves.

In my work, I have to do a lot of phone soliciting to get orders for my business. Calling someone I don't know and trying to get them to buy from me is a mental challenge. Recently I called a phone number and got someone who said they were not interested in our product or our services. They were rude and indifferent. When I got off the call, I had to separate the facts from the story.

My story could have been, "If I make any more prospecting calls, they are all going to reject my products or services. I bet that guy I just spoke to hates people like me."

How was I feeling now? Angry and depressed, and perhaps scared that I was not going to make enough money that month.

What were the facts?

- I called a number.
- A guy answered the phone.
- I introduced myself and my business.
- He said he wasn't interested.

So what is the positive self-talk story?

How about: "I have made thousands of calls in my career, and many of these calls resulted in customers or friends. Our products have helped many people and companies generate more revenue and navigate through difficult times. Surely this guy will be interested someday, but not today."

Look at the following chart. If we start with negative self-talk, we will create a negative feeling or emotion. This negative emotion will manifest itself in negative actions.

However positive self-talk will create a positive feeling, which will produce a positive behavior.

Likewise, neutral self-talk helps us suspend what we are telling ourselves so that we can control our feelings until we get more information about what we think is true or fictional.

Negative Self-Talk ➔	**Negative Feelings ➔**	*Negative Actions*

Positive Self-Talk ➔	**Positive Feelings ➔**	*Positive Actions*

Neutral Self-Talk ➔	**Controlled Feelings ➔**	*Logical Actions*

The first step toward controlling self-talk is to change the cycle. How is this done? First, we need to separate the facts from fiction, and then we need to change what we are telling ourselves based on those facts.

Let's go back to Mark's story. In his case, he closed his business. This is a fact. Negative self-talk would be: "My business closed down, therefore I am a loser, and everybody thinks I am a failure."

Positive self-talk would be: "My business closed down, but I am a smart guy with a master's degree and ten years of successful experience. I know there is a company out there that could benefit from this."

Neutral self-talk would be: "My business closed down. I need to get more information about what happened so I can learn something here."

My associate Suzi Streit shares the account of a traumatic event in her youth. When she was sixteen, her parents came to her and said the most terrible words any teenager could hear: "We're moving." The family had to transfer from Texas to Montgomery, Alabama. Suzi cried throughout the long car ride. She was miserable and made the journey miserable for everyone else in the car as well.

> **"What is important is not what happens to us, but how we respond to what happens to us."**
> *Jean-Paul Sartre*

Once in Montgomery, despite her mother's efforts to help her acclimate to her new hometown, Suzi refused to make friends, spending her free time in her room. A year went by before Suzi realized her negative self-story was keeping her from creating the life she really wanted.

"Years later, I thought about my behavior and felt intense shame for what I put my family through," Suzi says. "I lost a year of my life. I missed so many opportunities because I kept telling myself a fictional self-talk story of how bad it was."

Reflecting on Suzi's story, let's ask a few questions.

- What kind of story was she telling herself?
- What emotions did the story generate?
- What action did she take based on her emotions?
- What were the results?

What kind of story was Suzi telling herself? She was thinking that she would never make any friends. That her mom and dad didn't care how she felt. That she wasn't going to be happy in Alabama. That she was going to be miserable in the new place.

What emotions did this generate? Suzi felt hurt, lonely, sad, and depressed.

What actions did Suzi take? She withdrew from family activities and opportunities to discover new friends.

What were the results? She lost a year of her life and made the people around her suffer.

Facts, Opinions, and Fictional Stories

"Life is pulling a trick on me again," my friend said on a phone call one day. I asked him what he meant. He said he heard his company was going to reorganize and make some changes, so he was getting his résumé revised and ready. I asked him if he thought he would get fired. He said he was sure he would get cut in the first round of lay-offs. I asked him how he knew this to be true. He said he "just knew." I inquired about any evidence he might have. He simply said, "I just have a feeling."

The conversation between us was depressing. He was panicking and becoming overly fearful and cautious. He was an executive vice president at his company. I tried to get him to see that he could be wrong unless he validated what his "feelings" were telling him. "Feelings can be misleading," I said, "and the self-talk story you are creating from your feelings could be untrue." He said he knew he would be fired because this was a really strong feeling.

Can you see the difference between fact and a negative self-talk story? My friend "heard something" but didn't stop to see if what he heard was true. Now his feelings became so strong that he could not separate the facts from fiction.

Could my friend's story be true? Yes. It could also be completely false. However, he was hanging on to his negative self-talk story.

Why do we cling to our negative self-talk? Negative stories can be so strong that we act upon them. And when we rashly act without having all the facts, it can result in negative consequences for ourselves, our relationships, our jobs, etc.

Let's go back to the imagery from the movie *Castaway*. Imagine you are alone on an island. Your only desire is to get back home. You terribly miss the life you once had. Imagine the ocean tide brings in a Porta-Potty. There it is, on the sand, washed up on shore…a Porta-Potty. Negative self-talk and thinking could lead to missing an opportunity to use this material for a new idea. You could say to yourself, "OK God, is this the best you can do for me? Come on now…this is just crap." All you see is what it is, a toilet. However, positive self-talk and thinking would be very different and hopeful and say, "Oh God, thank you for this toilet. It's awesome. What can I do with this to create value and get me off this island?" Then you spend the rest of the day dancing instead of hiding under your bed sheets. Negative self-talk blinds you to the other opportunities right before your eyes.

"If you think you're too small to be effective, you have never been in bed with a mosquito."
Betty Reese

A key way to change our story is to separate the facts from the fictional story. When we make this separation, we can look at the events of our lives with unbiased observation.

What is a fact? A fact is something we can verify or prove. A fictional story is simply our opinion or a judgment. An opinion cannot be proven or verified. Facts can be proven and verified if they are true.

Here are some examples that can help you differentiate fact from fiction:

- "I was laid off from my job" (fact) versus "I was laid off because they don't like me" (fiction)
- "I got a low performance review" (fact) versus "Management is out to get me" (fiction)
- "My husband's Visa bill has an unknown hotel on it" (fact) versus "My husband is having an affair" (fiction)
- "My daughter has dyslexia" (fact) versus "My daughter has a disease that will ruin her future" (fiction)
- "My son failed a class" (fact) versus "My son is going be a failure at college and isn't mature enough to leave home" (fiction)

23

- "My dad bought my sister a more expensive car" (fact) versus "My dad favors her more than me" (fiction)
- "I wasn't picked for the soccer team" (fact) versus "I don't have any talents; I must be bad at everything" (fiction)

Here's another example. As you read, look for the facts and the fictional story in this incident from Suzi and her son Connor.

One evening Connor asked permission to play Nintendo. Suzi asked if he had done his homework, and he said yes. She told him he could play Nintendo. The next morning, as she was driving him to school, she looked in her rearview mirror and saw him frantically highlighting papers. Her blood pressure began to climb. Connor had not done his homework. He had lied to her, and he was going to get a bad grade on his paper.

Luckily for Connor, they were running late. Suzi told him with venom in her voice that they would "talk" when she picked him up. She watched him walk into the school with slumped shoulders and downcast eyes. She knew for sure he was guilty.

After she dropped him off, Suzi questioned her story and pulled out the facts.

- Connor said he did his homework.
- He played Nintendo.
- He was highlighting papers in the back seat.

The following were Suzi's assumptions, but they were not yet facts.

- Connor had not done his homework.
- Connor had lied.

- Connor was going to make a bad grade.
- Connor was guilty.

As Suzi questioned her facts, she started to calm down and become more rational. She thought of how happy and confident Connor had been when they left the house, compared to his body language as he walked into school. Could she possibly have caused that gloomy attitude by acting on the fictional story she had told herself?

When she picked Connor up, she stated the facts to him. "Connor, I asked you last night if your homework was done, and you said yes. Today on the way to school, I saw you hurriedly highlighting papers, and it makes me think that your homework really wasn't done. Am I right?"

Connor replied, "Mom, you're not right. I did finish my homework last night, but I needed to make an oral presentation based on my paper, so I made copies for everyone in my class. I decided at the last minute to highlight key sentences on each copy I was going to hand out."

Suzi could have saved herself the anxiety and stress of thinking her son was acting irresponsibly. She could have saved her son the frustration and disappointment he felt because his mother accused him of not doing his homework. We can save ourselves and the people in our lives so much pain if we just take the time to question our self-talk stories.

Facts can be verified or proved. Everything else is just a person's opinion or assumption that they attribute to what they hear or see. Many people hear opinions of someone else and create a whole new story about what they saw or heard. We do it so fast that many times we don't even realize we've done it.

Imagine you're at work and your self-talk story is, "This project is impossible. I'll never get it done." You think, "I feel overwhelmed and just don't feel like doing it." Or maybe you're going through the end of a relationship, and you're saying to yourself, "I'll never fall in love again." Or you have a troubled teenager and are thinking, "I'm a terrible parent. My kid hates me." If you change your self-talk, you will change how you feel. Change how you feel, and this will change your response and outlook. Ask yourself questions about what is fact and what is the fictional story you're telling yourself.

So instead of saying, "This project is impossible," try saying, "This project is important. Finishing it will be a huge accomplishment for me and the team." Instead of thinking, "I'll never fall in love again," try thinking, "My heart is open and I can receive new love when it is given." Instead of saying, "I'm a terrible parent," try saying, "I'm a good parent and will always be there for my kids."

Think about three of the most important goals you have for your life and consider how you talk to yourself about those goals. If you often consciously or subconsciously tell yourself, "I'll never [achieve that goal]" then you're right. You will most likely *never* accomplish any of your goals. What you tell yourself will determine how you feel. And how you feel will influence your attitude and actions, which will affect how your future unfolds.[1]

Summary

One day a business associate and friend brought some cookies to share with us at the office. The cookies looked and smelled so great. I couldn't wait to try one. However, after taking one bite I realized something just wasn't right. The cookie looked good but tasted poorly. To her dismay, my friend realized she left out a key ingredient in the recipe: salt.

To make delicious cookies, you need all the right ingredients. What you have read up to this point is one part of a recipe for thriving. This is just the beginning. Changing your thought process is a foundational ingredient like salt for a cookie or flour for a cake. You want to be sure you have everything you need. The rest of the book will give you all the ingredients you need to move from surviving to thriving.

Insight

Separating the Facts from Fiction

The fictional self-talk stories you're telling yourself keep you stuck in survival mode. They validate that the best you can do is simply get by.

Think about the greatest challenge you face right now. Take out a pen and a pad of paper, or get on the computer, and begin writing your story—complete with all the drama and emotion you feel about the events that have happened.

Ask:

- What am I telling myself—positive or negative—about what has happened?
- What is the worst that can happen? What is the best?
- Am I acting like the worst will happen to me?

Then make a list of the facts of your event, without any story, drama, or judgment. Read and reflect on your list as you ask yourself:

- Is this fact or fiction?
- What self-talk stories am I creating?
- What is the real story based on the facts?

Chapter Three

The Difference between Surviving and Thriving

A popular riddle goes like this: If a plane crashed on the border of Texas and Oklahoma, in which state would you bury the survivors?

At first the question stumps us, until we realize, "A-ha! You don't bury survivors!" However, when we respond to change by just surviving, we are, in a way, already buried, unable to get up and cross the border between surviving and thriving. Life's disappointments come in many forms. Like a plane crash, they can be disastrous. Often when I hear about others' disappointments, my first thought is to hope that they don't happen to me. So what kind of events can shake us up and send us into survival mode?

One day when I was a kid, my brother Rick was sound asleep on the couch in our living room. Seeing how peaceful he was sleeping, I decided to play a trick on him and watch what would happen. Up to this point, our after-school routine was to watch the TV show *The Three Stooges* just about every afternoon.

Getting a few ideas from this show, I went into the kitchen and found the large wooden kitchen matches. I took one match out, placed it between my brother's big toes, lit it, and ran into the garage. The garage door had a window so that I could watch just how long it took for my brother to wake up. The fire burned slowly down the match stick until it was grilling his toes. Like a bad dream, my brother began moaning, then woke up suddenly to find smoke rising from his feet. All I remember was how fast I moved to get out of the house when I heard my brother yell, "I'm going to kill you!" Running down the street, I was thinking how badly I needed to stay alive and survive until our parents got home, because otherwise my brother was going to bust me up.

I was definitely in survivor-mode then. However, as I became an adult I learned that real tragedies and circumstances can come our way that elicit just as much terror as I felt that day.

> **"I know God will not give me anything I can't handle.**
> **I just wish He didn't trust me so much."**
> *Mother Teresa*

For many, surviving has become a way of just getting by. When faced with a life challenge or uphill battle, surviving is the natural first stage of getting through difficulties. The quiet voice of the surviving mentality reminds you that you are doing well just getting through the day. It's like sitting on a bench in a busy city park on a sunny afternoon—wishing you were participating in what you see others do but never moving off the bench. Just sitting there, you feel safe; it's your spot, and familiarity keeps you warm and comfortable.

Besides, it's fun to observe, judge, and critique others' movements, mistakes, and motives. Other Survivors soon join you, and the group forms a Survivor club. The club even adopts a few rules for its members such as: "Everyone has to share a tragedy (over and over)." All members become skilled in living in the past while perfecting their position as self-appointed judges. It's a fun, comfortable club that becomes your support group. Meeting every week, all club members gather to watch others do life.

However, for some there is a nagging feeling that if they don't get off this bench and find a new club they are going to regret it. Sitting on the bench has become a slow death. And for many like me, there is a growing restlessness that there is something more. Sitting on the park bench was alright for a while. However, now it's time to move on, leave the comfort of my bench, give it up for someone else, and discover something new and more challenging.

Even so, there is a constant negative whisper that says, "Remember when you tried to move off the bench and you got hurt? It's safer just to sit here." Do you hear the voice that tells you to, "Go, try again, and reach for the stars"? And yet the other voice says, "You're going to get hurt again. Stay where you are—don't risk, don't fail. It's too painful." What kind of hurt, pain, and fears are we talking about?

Consider the following events and fears that have happened to friends and people around me. Stories like these may be familiar to you or to someone close to you.

- John and Ann return home from a nice night out together. They get a call at midnight that their forty-year-old son has dropped dead from a heart attack.

- Danny knew he was spending more than his income would allow. Now the debt is so large that all his money goes to pay interest. Depression and despair rob him of his sleep.

- Karen, Steve, and their five children are enjoying their beautiful home. The next day, a tornado rips apart their neighborhood. They are now homeless.

- Joanne is a highly successful CEO of a leading corporation. However, revenue has dropped dramatically. She tells her executive team that the company is going to make drastic cuts and that their survival is on the line.

- Jodie and Robert love their church and are particularly grateful for the youth program. Then their daughter tells them a church staff member has been molesting her.

- Lily, a single mom of three, finally has a job that pays the mortgage. After one month, she's told that the plant is closing and that, as the newest employee, she will be the first to go.

- Mark started his own dream business four years ago, but the market is changing and his clients are disappearing. Bankruptcy sounds like his only option.

- Angie, a hospital nurse and avid volunteer, has always been a tower of support for her patients and community. She finds out she has stage-four cancer.

- As she does every day, Rebecca kisses her husband good-bye and sends him off to work. Two hours later, she sees on the news that the building he works in has collapsed from a terrorist attack.

- Nancy has a vision of a happy family. However, her husband is an alcoholic who refuses help.

- Bill is an executive at a large financial services company. He expects next year's revenues to drop twenty percent and is looking to make significant personal cuts and weather the storm.

- Sean has worked hard for twenty-two years. He finds out that management has been "cooking the books," the company is worthless, and he's out of a job—and a pension.

These kinds of life-altering challenges plunge us into survival, the first phase of recovery. Survival is good! But it's meant to be a beginning point, not an ending. What is the difference between surviving and thriving in these events?

When we're surviving, we do what we can just to get by. We're in shock, on autopilot. We haven't checked out of life, but we haven't checked back in, either. When we get into bed each night, it's hard to remember what happened that day. We feel an overwhelming sense of loss and despair. Sometimes it's easier to stay stuck in our darkness than it is to turn on the light.

> **"It is nothing to die. It is an awful thing never to have lived."**
> *Jean Valjean, from Victor Hugo's* Les Miserables

One of the biggest differences I see between Survivors and Thrivers is that Thrivers bounce back better than before. They have a kind of super-resilience. They may feel fear, but they choose to have courage, focusing on capabilities and not excuses. Unlike Survivors, who feel that life happens *to* them and that the best they can do is dodge bullets and put out fires, Thrivers charge into the flames of life without blaming others for their circumstances. They are fully engaged, even while managing a crisis. One foot is grounded in the realities of the present, but the other foot is already stretched into the possibilities of the future. Here are two scenarios showing the difference between surviving and thriving.

Richard, age 55, lost his job after fifteen years of service. At his age, it's going to be hard to get another job anytime soon. After three months, he is still blaming the company management and their incompetency for his circumstance. His friends began avoiding him because they were tired of hearing Richards's constant complaining and opinion about how he was the victim.

Angie, age 55, discovered she has cancer and spent days crying and weeping. As she began to acknowledge the reality of her situation, she grieved the loss and pain of her current life but accepted her new life. Joining a cancer support group and relying on the help of family and friends, she is learning all she can about her medical problem. Now she is helping others with the same problem, giving them hope and encouragement.

In both cases, Richard and Angie are surviving life. However, Angie is going beyond just surviving. She is thriving in her situation. Imagine that you were having coffee with both Richard and Angie. Which one would you want to listen to? Which one is fighting back like a sparrow in a hurricane?

Are you going through a difficult time? Survivor thinking is natural and good. You need to restore and heal during these times. Park benches are good. I love them when I am tired and need a rest. However, when Survivors are sitting on the bench, they may be there too long and not know it. Maybe you realize you have been sitting on the bench too long. Can you hear the subtle, constant whisper that says, "It's time to get off the bench"?

What's the difference between Survivors and Thrivers? Survivors look for the park bench, but Thrivers are making parks and benches for others to take a rest.

Four Behaviors

Survivors and Thrivers behave in distinctly different ways, as illustrated in the chart on page 38. One behavior exhibits specific characteristics of a Survivor. The other behavior describes a Thriver's more positive characteristics.

The purpose of these Survivor-Thriver characteristics is to help you see where you are in your life. You may not resonate with each description, but you may discover that one or two of these descriptions fit your situation. Hopefully, the chart will help you identify where you are and will help you make the adjustments needed to "get off the bench" and discover a new world.

Train Dodging

I once took an Amtrak train ride from Dallas to San Antonio. The trip took about ten hours and included a prime rib dinner in the dining car. The private cabin we were in was tiny but comfortable. The bed and a small chair folded down from the wall. The ride on the way down was worth the money. However, when I got to San Antonio, the experience was enough. I didn't want to go back the same way!

So, I decided to take a Southwest flight back to Dallas and avoid the train. On the way back home I was thinking about the number of people who are killed by trains each year. The impact of a train would be devastating. However, have you ever wondered how people get in the way of a train? When I was on my trip, it had seemed like the train was blowing the whistle every ten minutes if not more.

Dodging life's challenges is like getting out of the way of a train coming down the tracks. For those who get in the way of the train, the impact is life-changing for everyone involved. Consider for a moment that the train is named "Change" and it brings with it life's challenges and surprises. How does someone get hit by this train? I have found that the "Change" train comes at me two ways.

1. Didn't have a clue! I just woke up one day and found myself on the tracks. I didn't know how or why I got there. I didn't even see it coming. However, by the time I realized that the train was going to hit me, it was too late. No time to analyze an escape, just *wham!* Like the time I got a surprise letter from the IRS. Or finding out your spouse left you for someone else and you never saw it coming.

2. Tied myself up and laid down in front of the train. Sounds stupid, I know. I have made some bad choices and didn't follow the advice I got from people who knew what this train looked like. Like forgetting I need to get my registration

and inspection sticker replaced, or filing my taxes late. It's like ignoring a speeding ticket, not paying bills on time and having to pay late fees, or not studying for a test at college. This list seems to get bigger, too.

The "Change" train is coming! Either you get in its way or you just find yourself on the tracks. What you do next is what this book is about. In the next few chapters we will look at the difference between the behaviors of a Survivor and Thriver. Let's review those categories now.

Self-Preservation vs. Self-Growth

Are you struggling with a surprising life challenge? Have you been run over yet? If so, then you are in self-preservation. Currently still in shock, you just can't make sense out of it. You may be asking yourself, "Why me?" You are likely feeling somewhat helpless, unsure, and withdrawn. However, maybe you are far enough down the road after the train has passed that you have a very clear assessment of the damage. You have had some time to heal and adjust. And now you desire to be more engaged with life and fight back, risk again. You are making the switch to more of a thriving mode. When you're more certain of your direction, your confidence and decisions empower you.

Victim vs. Warrior

Victims are everywhere. Turn on the news and discover someone was robbed, swindled, or raped. It wasn't their fault; someone else did this to them. They are, in fact, the victims. Being a victim in a surviving mode is to be expected. As victims, we blame someone else for our misfortune. We feel hopeless and our security is shattered—

all of which is accompanied by lots of emotion. These are some of the signs that you are still in a surviving mode. After some time, if you're not careful, you will get stuck at this phase. To move to a more thriving mode, you begin to make the transition to a warrior. Thrivers are warriors who understand that they are accountable to themselves to discipline their thinking and to shape their future and the future of those around them. There is a determination to win and conquer despite the loss. With each step, they are more logical and realistic in their ways, plans, and actions.

Parasite vs. Player

Initially when a crisis happens, it's also natural to become needier. Our behaviors become more reactive and, like a hurt animal, we may bite if provoked. We attach ourselves to those people or systems that can help us, much like parasites. We don't have enough energy of our own, so we absorb all we can get from others. Soon we find that we feed off the sympathy of others, talking about the past, going over and over in our minds what happened. Players, in contrast, are those who move from the parasite mode to a more active, assertive mode. We want to get back into the game again and start to create energy for ourselves and others. Players have a more proactive approach to life. Gone is the need to review the past mistakes or hurts. Not to ignore the past, but to learn more from what happened so we can become better players.

Actor vs. Director

Survivors tend to be actors on stage while Thrivers take charge and run the production. Actors tend to act when someone says, "Action!" At times, their real identity is hidden or unclear. Having a present focus but not looking at the entire production is the role

37

of an actor. These characteristics are not bad but somewhat natural to the surviving mode. However, if you are not careful, you may find that after many years you're still in Survivor/Actor role. Thrivers, as we will see, are more like directors. Endless possibilities are before them, accompanied by a "can do" attitude. They focus on the future with a clear picture of their strengths and weaknesses.

Surviving Versus Thriving:
The Four Behaviors

<u>*Surviving*</u>		<u>*Thriving*</u>
1. Self-Preservation	**vs.**	**Self-Growth**
- Shocked		- Healing
- Withdrawn		- Engaged
- Helpless		- Empowered
2. Victim	**vs.**	**Warrior**
- Blaming		- Accountable
- Hopeless		- Determined
- Emotional		- Logical
3. Parasite	**vs.**	**Player**
- Passive		- Assertive
- Energy-absorbing		- Energy-producing
- Reactive		- Proactive
4. Actor	**vs.**	**Director**
- Can't be done		- Can be done
- Present-focused		- Future-focused
- Unclear identity		- Clear identity

Summary

Look at the chart on the previous page. All four characteristic are listed. Our adventure starts by looking at each one and discovering where you are in life. What changes need to be made to get you to the next level? As you reflect on the differences between the four behaviors, consider which category you would say most often describes you and your reaction to crises or challenges. In the next few chapters, we will take a look at how these different behaviors play out—each chapter will discuss a different pair of contrasting behaviors. What you read in the next chapter will teach you some surprising differences between self-preservation and self-growth and why self-preservation mode doesn't protect us as much as it robs us of our right to heal.

Insight

Carrots, Eggs, and Coffee Beans (Author Unknown)

Just as different foods respond differently in hot water, the same can be said of people.

What happens when you put carrots in a pot of boiling water? How about eggs or coffee beans? When we fill three pots with water—put carrots in the first, eggs in the second, and coffee beans in the third—then turn up the heat, we see that different things happen. The carrots go in strong and hard but soften when they're boiled. The eggs stay hard on the outside, but their soft insides stiffen. Yet the coffee beans don't change their form or texture. Instead, they release a part of themselves to change their surroundings—filling the water and the air with their essence.

Let's face it. Painful personal trauma and tragedy—like illness or injury, death of a loved one, loss of a job, or the unexpected breakup of a relationship—are unavoidable. The question is: Will these private calamities erode our capacity to be happy or cause us to become stronger and better able to live a meaningful and fulfilling life?

Some people start out with strength like the carrots but wilt in the face of adversity. When faced with a loss or other trial, the Survivor's spirit is like the inside of an egg: hardship "hard boils" their heart. Others are coffee beans, infusing the world with their inner richness when the heat is on.

Ask yourself: How do I respond when I'm in hot water? Am I a carrot, an egg, or a coffee bean?

Chapter Four

Self-Preservation Versus Self-Growth

When I was fifteen, my friend Larry and I were on a motorcycle together as we returned from a church function. We were cruising down Spring Valley Road in Richardson, Texas, which had four lanes and a clear view for miles. Our destination was a local pizza place. Little did I know that I would never get there. Without warning, a drunk driver pulled out in front of us. We hit the car going fifty-five miles an hour.

Like a missile, Larry went through the driver's side window, hitting the driver and anything else in the way with his helmet. I slammed into the car door, flew off the bike, hit my helmeted head, flew straight up in the air, did a few flips, and ended up on the roof of the passenger's side like I was sitting in a chair. My ears were ringing. When I opened my eyes, everything was spinning. I jumped off the car and immediately fell to the ground, certain that something was broken.

When I hit the ground, I realized there was no damage that I could see or feel. I was thankful my legs and arms were intact. I walked over to the grass to lie down. Then I went into shock— completely delirious and irrational shock. The world was spinning.

My words were slurred. I remember trying just to get a handle on where I was and what happened. It all seemed so unreal.

I remember saying to myself, "Am I dead? I'm not dead. Everything's OK. I'm going to be fine. I think I will walk home. What about my homework? Is it dinnertime? What time is it? Where is Larry? Do I have any brain damage?"

A few minutes later, the ambulance arrived. I didn't want anyone touching me and was trying to act like I was fine. I am sure the paramedics knew I was in shock. Both of us were wearing helmets, which saved our lives. Upon arrival at the hospital, we were released with minor cuts and a few stitches.

After we left the hospital, I got permission to spend the night with Larry at his house. His mom came in every ten minutes to check on us, making sure we didn't have any brain damage.

The accident brought an immediate change in our life plan, though Larry and I responded in dramatically different ways. I couldn't sleep. My thoughts were on what could have happened, how bad the wreck could have been, and how fortunate I was to be alive. Getting on another motorcycle was the last thing I wanted to do. After a few hours, Larry asked me how I was doing. I replied that I was OK and asked him how he was doing. Larry said, "I'm going to talk to my dad about getting a bigger bike and a better helmet, and maybe a protective jacket." At the time, I thought he must be crazy. However, Larry was already past the survivor stage and on the way to thriving. In contrast, the first thing I wanted to do was to keep from getting hurt again. I didn't want to experience a motorcycle wreck again. I was in self-preservation mode.

Survivors Focus on Self-Preservation

Preservation—defined as protecting from harm and danger—is a natural survival technique. Our brains unleash an array of chemicals and hormones that shield us from more danger.

When a turtle is frightened or threatened, it rapidly retreats into its shell. In self-preservation mode, we go into our shell, like a turtle, where it's safe. We don't want to experience the next bad thing. Therefore, when something bad happens to you, you can expect to go into some form of self-preservation. However, Larry was past self-preservation and already focused on the opposite: self-growth, which is a characteristic of Thrivers. He was thinking about the next ride and what he learned from his experience. Not me. I was thinking about how bad the accident could have been and how much I didn't want to experience another wreck.

> **"Do not pray for tasks equal to your powers,
> but pray for power equal to your tasks."**
> *Bishop Phillip Brooks*

Dodging Danger

Shock causes us to freeze the use of our gifts and talents because all we can focus on is dodging danger. A violent collision or a heavy blow causes the shock we feel. It's natural to protect ourselves from this pain.

There is a difference between physical shock and emotional shock. For instance, physical shock like my motorcycle accident caused trauma to my body from the sudden impact of the collision. Trauma to the body can heal over time. However, emotional shock happens when you experience sudden change in things like finances, lose a job or a loved one, or discover that a spouse is unfaithful. In my accident, for example, I struggled more from the emotional shock than the physical shock. After a few days, the physical scars healed and were barely visible. However, recovering from emotional trauma may take years.

Most people don't like loss or pain. I know I don't. If we can, we want to avoid or escape it. However, pain has a benefit: it can chase the foolishness out of us. It has a way of causing us to see which priorities are important and which are not. At the same time, it creates a life experience, a reference point to self-preserve in the future so we don't get hurt again. For example, in the early stages of a divorce many people strongly believe that they will never remarry again. My experience was much the same. I was determined I would never remarry. Although I am not remarried today, I have changed my mind on the matter. Indeed someday I would like to remarry. The difference is that when we are hurt we initially want to keep from getting hurt again. Therefore, we throw up brick walls around our emotions in order to protect ourselves. This is a normal process to survive the event.

However, if we're not careful, we can get stuck in self-preservation. It's our nature to find comfort in things that remain the same—from jobs to friendships to relationships. We resist change out of the fear that if we let go of what we know, we'll face circumstances we can't handle. Nevertheless, in the end, staying in self-preservation mode doesn't protect us as much as it robs us of our right to heal. It also robs us of our ability to realize our dreams. Self-preservation, though an important stage in healing, causes us to grow comfortable with our situation. If we don't see it for what it is, we can't move forward.

People are stuck in self-preservation if they are:

- Not questioning the way things are for fear of change and risk.
- Not being open to love because of a previous relationship.
- Not doing something they love because of a past hurt.

Following are some examples of this behavior:

- Not getting married again because of a painful divorce.
- Not starting a business because of a past business failure.
- Not making new friends because of hurt or rejection from past relationships.
- Not going to church because of a bad experience with a church leader.

> **"You play the hand you're dealt.**
> **I think the game's worthwhile."**
> *C.S. Lewis*

Losing the Dream

I graduated from college with a degree in Electrical Power Distribution and Control from Northlake Junior College in December and landed a job with Genesis Electronics Company the same month. However, a year later I found myself wanting to pursue my own dreams of starting my own business. I had an idea I kept thinking about—selling mini-blinds for office buildings—and wanted to give it a try. I did some homework, and a few months later I got the courage to take the risk and quit my job to start a new business. I was newly married, living in a trailer park on a nice lake close to town. I had a vision of one day owning a custom home and a boat. My goal was to increase my income, and I was hoping this idea would get me there. Many of my friends and family were excited about the new direction in my life, while others found fault with my decision.

There were many reasons not to start my own business, the biggest one being the fear I had that it wouldn't work. One day, I outlined on a napkin the pros and cons of starting my own business. I discovered that the potential opportunity outweighed the possible problems. Once I realized this, I quit my job and launched into my marketing plan. In just a few months I landed my first sale and contract! Soon I got another contract, and then another, with builders of apartments and office buildings. The business grew, employees were added, and after three years we bought one of our competitors. In a short time, things were going better than I had ever imagined!

After a few years, we had seven retail stores and our own manufacturing plant. I gained a lot of respect from our circle of friends and professional contacts because of our aggressive business approach. I couldn't imagine life being any better. I remember singing a song from one of the Scrooge movies I saw that went, "I like life and life likes me." This song kind of summed up how my life was at that time. Little did I know that a dark train of change was headed my way.

Most of our products were with the building industry, while the balance of sales came through our retail stores. Four years into this business, the banking industry was going through a shake-up. The savings and loan companies had been loaning money to develop large commercial properties for several years until the news stories began to break about the deceptive loan practices and inflated property values. The banking economy began to shift, and things didn't work out as I had hoped. Builders that I had contracts with filed for bankruptcy. I remember receiving five bankruptcy notices in one week, totaling almost a million dollars in receivables for my business. My team and I worked hard to try to salvage the business, but every day brought more bad news.

To make matters worse, after we had downsized from seven store locations to two, I got news from a travel agency thanking me for sending my financial controller to the Bahamas. The truth was that I hadn't sent my controller to the Bahamas. He was supposed to be in the hospital; a few weeks earlier, our controller requested time off from work so he could spend a few days in the hospital for a series of tests. I didn't have any reason to think he was being deceptive. While we were scrambling to resolve the current situation, we discovered our controller was embezzling money and forging checks. He disappeared, leaving me to deal with a business that had little to no financial reserves.

What a nightmare! However, things continued to go from bad to worse. After a downsized business and an employee embezzlement, I spotted an article in the newspaper highlighting my accomplishments in the mini-blind business. Horrible timing! The depression I felt was of an incredible magnitude. I lost more than a business and money; I lost friends and self-esteem. The friends who celebrated my success were not there for me when the business went down the drain. After selling off most of the business, I ended up getting a job working for a painter. One day I was a successful businessman, and the next day I was on my knees painting baseboards. The only hope that kept me going was my religious faith and the birth of my first son. I had to keep going forward for my new family.

The disappointment and hurt from losing my company was an experience I would never forget. I was going to enter self-

47

preservation mode to keep from experiencing this again. Problems with the IRS reminded me of this incident for years. I made myself a promise: I would never go into business for myself again. And for fifteen years I kept that promise. Why? Not for lack of ideas. I didn't try again because I was focused on self-preservation. The emotional shock and pain of failing was very real, and this pain was what I wanted to avoid.

Getting Stuck

We all have dreams—from starting our own business, to falling in love, to raising a family, to traveling around the world. Life's dreams are endless. We dream and launch them into reality, hoping it will all work out. Often, though, it doesn't. Disappointment is followed by depression. What do we do? We self-preserve. The walls go up, especially around the disappointing experience or event. We avoid dealing with it, even avoid learning from it. Now we're stuck.

A man I know was devastated when his spouse had an affair. The impact was, as one would expect, traumatic. Yet ten years later he is still telling people he is in the healing process. Is this guy stuck? He sure is, and he doesn't know it. This man is stuck in self-preservation mode. For him to move forward, he needs to grieve the loss, discover what he learned, and avoid bringing the past up at every conversation. Counseling would be good medicine for him, too. If I broke my arm, I would see a doctor who would put a cast on it. After a healing period, the cast comes off. The arm gets worked out and back to normal. Is this painful? Yes! But it doesn't mean one must keep wearing the cast.

The mental cast is good for a time, but at some point the cast needs to come off. The person who is still healing after ten years is stuck in self-preservation mode. Imagine the infection (not to mention the muscle atrophy) keeping a cast on your arm ten years after you broke it would create! It sounds ridiculous. Yet counseling offices are filled with people who are stuck in a mental cast.

Thrivers Focus on Self-Growth

One of the ways we can avoid getting stuck in self-preservation is to focus on self-growth. It's easier to stay in self-preservation, but in order to thrive we need to heal and grow.

When we move into self-growth mode, we begin to take control of our circumstances. Instead of looking back at what happened to us and what we lost, we begin to look ahead to see the possibilities. In self-growth, we gain a refreshed sense of who we are and what we have control over. We "own it." This ownership helps us look the experience in the face and deal with some important issues.

The move from self-preservation to self-growth starts by grieving the loss and embracing what you have gained from this event. Begin by talking with your close friends about what you learned from this experience. "Treasure hunt" these experiences—in other words, look for the valuable positive lessons you learned during these situations. Ask yourself questions like:

- Am I growing in relationship to this event?
- What could I do differently?
- What am I responsible for?
- What am I not responsible for?
- Am I blaming others?
- What are the fictional stories I am telling myself?
- Am I avoiding the role of the victim?
- Am I avoiding the feeling of helplessness? (Or, do I feel helpless?)

49

- Am I talking to my friends over and over about the miserable experience?

- Are my conversations about my past or more about my future?

In a financial loss, we must admit what part we played in our undoing. For a while, all I wanted to talk about was the failed business. Eventually I began to take responsibility for what I could have done differently about the controller who stole money from my company. For instance, I could have audited the books more often. I could have set up a process of checks and balances to keep employees from attempting to steal. I accepted where I was and how I got there. I began telling friends what I had learned from this experience.

Maybe your marriage failed, and your spouse left you. You thought you would never get divorced. Do you find you are frequently discussing this event? Repeatedly renewing the pain about what happened? When you are in conversation with friends and family, pay close attention to what you are saying. Do you find that most of the conversations that you initiate are about your pain? Self-growth causes you to take ownership for your part.

Making the mental shift to self-growth kick-starts us into evaluating our options. Of course, it's easier to stay where we are; even when it's depressing and unhealthy, at least we know what to expect. However, self-growth forces us to climb the mountain even when we don't want to.

> **"Facing it—always facing it—that's the way to get through. Face it!"**
> *Joseph Conrad*

When we are in self-preservation mode, we retreat from facing our circumstances. When we are in self-growth mode, we can look at our pain. We stop asking, "Why me?" and start mining for nuggets of the wisdom gained through our experiences that can help ourselves and others. Why are we fearful? What fictional story are we telling ourselves? What do we need to do to overcome this?

For years after my motorcycle accident, whenever I saw a car darting into the street, I felt the same panic and fear. I didn't want to be on a motorcycle ever again. I thought, "Hey, I didn't ask for this experience; it just happened." I had survived the accident but was still stuck in the fear that it caused. For several years, I didn't want anything to do with Spring Valley Road or motorcycles.

My personal victory was to buy a Honda 350 motorcycle and cruise down Spring Valley Road once again! Could I have another accident? Yes, I could. But I also could ride for years without anything happening. Our perceptions are shaped by our experience. To overcome this challenge, I had to come to terms with my fear of what could happen, which was being fed by my fictional story. To begin, I took a motorcycle riding class and became better informed about how to ride a bike more defensively. Educating myself helped. I also decided why I was fearful. I admitted, "I am fearful of getting on a motorcycle because I will have another accident."

That was a fictional story: "I will have another accident." The truth is that more accidents happen in cars than motorcycles when you look at the population of cars versus motorcycles. Also, how did I know "I will" have another accident? I didn't really know. However, telling myself this had me acting like I would indeed have another accident. The truth is that I *could* have an accident, but I could also *not* have an accident. I decided that my fear was keeping me from what I enjoyed. My fictional story fed my fear. So, kill the story and kill the fear.

By dealing with the fear my experience created and understanding my fictional story, I could change my perception—and again enjoy the joys of motorcycle riding. Was this easy? No, it was an exercise in mental discipline. Speaking of amazing people who use discipline to reshape their life.

Kindred Stories

My friend Debbie is a good example of a person moving from self-preservation to self-growth. Several years ago, Debbie went through a serious surgery to remove an AVM (arteriovenous malformation) from her brain. An AVM is a "tangling" of blood vessels in the brain that can cause many symptoms, including a hemorrhage.

After the surgery, Debbie could remember waking up from the anesthesia with many doctors hovering over her bed. The medical staff was asking her lots of questions, prompting her to move her legs, arms, and fingers and to answer simple questions about herself. It all seemed so easy until she realized that she couldn't respond to many of their questions in the way that she had before surgery. Her brain wasn't the same, and her body wasn't either. She couldn't speak and couldn't feel or move the left side of her body. Debbie recalls:

> Even though my speech and half of my body were extremely different, I was alive. I remembered my past: who my first-grade teacher was, where I went to church, and all of my family and friends. That's what was most important to me, and I was peaceful. I knew I had a big job ahead of me, but I could do it because the part of my brain that held all of my memory was perfect. So my month-long hospital stay began with intense occupational, physical, and speech therapy.

The days in the hospital and rehab unit seemed long sometimes because I missed my husband and eight-year-old son, but I knew I would get better. I knew that I didn't want to spend many more days in a wheelchair, dependent on others for even my most basic needs. So here I am now, walking on my own and taking care of my teenage son and myself. I work and take college classes part-time. And even though my husband and I separated and eventually divorced just a year after my life-changing surgery, I am peaceful, happy, and, most of all, thankful for all the blessings I have in my family and friends and the joy I have in my life. Even though I will never again have normal function of my left arm and leg, I feel blessed. God is with me every day.

As I listened to Debbie's story, I kept wondering what I would have done. What would you do? When I asked Debbie what her first thought was when she discovered she was paralyzed, she said, "I was lucky. I still had my right side."

Debbie's self-growth helps her stay focused on healing and learning—with the insight that she has a life yet to be lived. She could be bitter, a victim of fate, but instead, she has moved from Survivor to Thriver. She has a "Let's look at what I *do* have, not what I *don't* have" perspective. Debbie had a strong reliance on a higher power—her Christian belief in God—and that was part of her ability to move forward.

> **"Most people never run far enough on their first wind to find out they've got a second. Give your dreams all you've got and you'll be amazed at the energy that comes out of you."**
> *William James*

Another sign that you are in self-growth is when you begin to share your experience with the goal of helping others who are going through a similar situation. People who are hurting are comforted by hearing from people who have been through a similar situation. If you found yourself having to recover from being paralyzed from a surgery, with whom do you want to talk? I would want to talk with someone who went through the same experience and came out a winner. I would want to talk with someone like Debbie!

Propellers and Friends, Not Anchors

Self-growth helps you assess your friends—whether they are helping you move on or helping you stay stuck. It's true what they say about misery: it does love company!

Suzi shares these words of wisdom that have helped her along the way: "Surround yourself with people who are propellers, not anchors. Think of what an anchor does for a boat: it holds it in place and keeps it from moving. A propeller stirs the water and moves the boat forward. Anchors tell you what you *want* to hear; propellers tell you what you *need* to hear. Anchors hold you down while propellers move you to a new place. In self-growth, it is good to take an inventory of the friends and family members who are either your propellers or anchors. Self-growth mode helps to identify the anchors in our lives and replace them with propellers."

After the break-up of my marriage, I joined a divorce recovery group. Although most people in the group had been divorced for two to three years, I soon discovered that some of them were "anchored" in self-preservation. Why? It felt safer to not move on. And they enjoyed the sympathy they received from the rest of the group.

Others in the group, however, were "propellers"—they were moving forward in their lives. And these were the people with whom I chose to connect. They helped propel me out of self-preservation and into self-growth.

Summary

Let's review our chart below that contrasts Surviving and Thriving to understand more about the difference between the two. In this chapter, we've discovered the negative characteristics associated with self-preservation: shock, withdrawal, and a focus on our own helplessness. In contrast, when we focus on self-growth, we experience healing, we engage in life and see our circumstance for what it is, and we feel empowered.

Surviving		*Thriving*
Self-Preservation	vs.	**Self-Growth**
- Shocked		- Healing
- Withdrawn		- Engaged
- Helpless		- Empowered

The next chapter will challenge you to evaluate and determine another aspect of your typical reaction to your circumstances when your world is falling apart. You will learn how to recognize and reverse the "victim" mentality and discover specific key ways to develop a "warrior" approach to victory over your circumstances.

Insight

Self-Preservation Versus Self-Growth

Ask yourself these questions:

- Am I stuck in self-preservation?
- What experience have I had in the past that is still holding me back?
- Do I frequently discuss my crisis in a way that keeps me stuck?
- Are my friends anchoring me in self-preservation or propelling me toward self-growth?
- What am I doing to move forward and grow?

Chapter Five

Victim Versus Warrior

One steamy, midsummer day a man approached me at my office. He told me that his station wagon had broken down. He said he was from South Texas and that his wife and seven kids were waiting back at his car. They were on their way to a relative's house that was still many hours away. He said he needed money to buy a carburetor so they could continue to their destination.

I asked the man how much a new part for his car would cost. He said about eighty dollars for a used part. I wasn't sure what to do. The fictional story I was telling myself was that this "bum" was playing me for a fool. He was playing a helpless victim role to get money from unsuspecting people. Yet he was persistent, and his story seemed believable. Maybe he had a real need and a real problem, and he was doing what he could to resolve the issue. I hesitantly opened my cash register in the store and gave the man enough money to buy the parts he needed.

The man thanked me over and over. When he left, I decided to follow him, just far enough behind so that he wouldn't see me. Less than a block down the street, as I came around the corner of an office building, I spotted a car in the middle of a parking lot. In it were a woman and seven kids, who seemed to range in age from one to ten. The woman was holding a baby. They all looked like they had been waiting for some time. The windows were rolled down, the car hood was open, and on the ground was a bunch of car parts.

At that moment, I was so glad that I had done something to help. This young father of seven was just doing what he could to get through a difficult situation. I didn't sense that he was blaming everyone else for the problem. He could have blamed the manufacturer, the mechanic, a family member, and so on. However, he simply explained what had happened and asked for my help. The point is, if I had held on to a victim story, I would have responded to this man's need differently. The man who needed a carburetor could have maintained the self-story of a victim: "Oh, I'm helpless, nobody wants to help me." I'm glad he didn't.

Survivors Focus on Being Victims

I find that people who are in need have two choices.

1. Play a victim, helpless, or villain role (Victim)
2. Take ownership and ask for help (Warrior)

Have you ever played a victim role? Have you ever had a problem and played a helpless role? Have you ever had a life problem and blamed everyone else or spent hours on the phone talking to everyone who will listen to your story about the villain in your life? I have many times. Once I overslept and didn't show up to work on time. My boss asked me why I was late. I said it was the fault of my alarm clock. The clock was the villain, and I was the victim. It was a pretty good story, too. So good that it kept me from owning up to my responsibilities. To be honest, I had been late several times to work before. When you play a victim role, you can create all kinds of stories. These stories allowed me to feel good about my bad work habits. However, if you can understand what these stories look like, then you will be able to minimize their effects.

In victim mode, we tell ourselves one of three stories.

The first is the victim story:

> "It's not my fault. I am an innocent suffering person. I had good intentions."

The second is the villain story:

> "It's your fault. You did it to me. You're responsible for my pain and suffering."

The third is the helpless story:

> "There's nothing I can do. No matter what I do, it won't work."

In the previous chapter, we spoke about propellers and anchors. These victim roles truly keep us anchored to our problems, while breaking out of this mindset propels us to see other opportunities.

Permission to Do Nothing

When we take on the role of a victim, we give ourselves permission to do absolutely nothing. If there's nothing we can do, why bother? When we are surviving an event, we have a tendency to play a victim role. The slip into this role can be as subtle as a cat stalking a mouse. If you're cautious, you can keep it from sneaking up on you. And if you listen carefully to what you're saying, the victim role is easy to identify.

Victim stories entice us and suck us in, like a worm on a hook that tempts a hungry fish to take the bait. Radio talk shows are built on this "hungry fish" deception. We are attracted to victim stories, sad stories we can all relate to. For instance, I once heard a caller on a radio talk show who said her husband had been looking at women on the Internet. She started her story in tears. I could hear and feel the wife's hurt, and I felt badly for her. Her hurt was real, and the story seemed true. I found myself mad at her husband even though I didn't know him. I was completely sucked in. However, what the radio host did next surprised me. She didn't empathize with this woman at all, like I would have. She asked her a direct and very hard question about what *she* had done to contribute to the problem of her husband getting intimacy through cybersex.

At first the woman wanted to stay focused on her "I'm a victim" story. She was convinced she was innocent and helpless, and her husband was the villain. She stuttered and stumbled through her words while the radio host asked her the same question again. Eventually she admitted to displaying "explosive anger" and often saying hurtful things to her husband.

Believing the victim, villain, or helpless story is a crutch that we use over and over. We tell ourselves that there's nothing we can do, we believe it, and we feel helpless. We act helpless, too. We have one perspective, and that is to see our situation as hopeless.

Consider a wife whose husband runs away with a younger woman. She is the victim of ultimate rejection. She can justify her bitterness and anger toward her husband or the other woman. The victim position keeps her stuck. The other woman becomes the villain and she, as the victim, is helpless to do anything to fix her situation. She is frequently sad and depressed, and because of the divorce she has to work and cannot stay at home with her kids. This is the fault of the villain (the husband or the other woman).

She is swimming in debt, the kids want this and that, but it's "Dad's fault" that they have to do without. She perceives that other people have better lives, jobs, cars, and houses like she used to have, but the fact that she doesn't have these things is all the fault of the villain and his new wife.

Can you blame her? Would you feel the same way? What would happen if she keeps her attention and focus on being the victim?

These victim stories do more to sustain her bitterness, which will affect her relationships with others. What she needs to do to move forward and out of this mode is to recognize that the clever victim stories are keeping her stuck. She can start by asking herself questions to determine what type of role she is using.

Victim Role:

- Am I acting like I am an innocent sufferer?
- Am I ignoring the role that I played in contributing to the problem?
- What are my true intentions?

Villain Role:

- Am I ascribing negative motives to the other person?
- Am I exaggerating my own innocence?
- Am I overemphasizing the other person's guilt?
- Am I dehumanizing the other person by making unfair generalizations?
- Am I giving excuses for my bad behavior?

Helpless Role:

- Am I assuming there is no alternative to our predicament?

- Do I spend more time explaining why I can't do anything to change my situation than looking for solutions?
- Do I believe I cannot change my behavior, skills, or traits?

When we are living as a victim, we stay stuck in survival mode and avoid going beyond surviving into a more thriving mode. When in a crisis, the natural response is to put all the blame on someone else. All our energy goes into playing the blame game. The irony is that in this game, we always lose. Victim, villain, and helpless stories bring us down and keep us stuck.

> "Good thoughts and actions can never produce bad results; bad thoughts and actions can never produce good results. This is but saying that nothing can come from corn but corn, nothing from nettles but nettles."
> *As A Man Thinketh by James Allen*

Avoid the Victim, Villain, and Helpless Stories

As I indicated, there is more to my earlier story about accepting an old friend's job offer that later went south. It taught me a lot about playing the victim. As I said, my loyalty to a friend in need, along with a healthy dose of prayer, led me to accept his offer over another equally appealing opportunity.

I started in May as part of the executive team. We had our first meeting with the company's investors three months later in August. When I left that investor meeting, I felt sick. I knew the investors were not interested in a company that was two years old and hadn't met one financial projection. They had already lost their confidence in the CEO. As expected, the investors pulled their funding, putting the company in financial hardship. Later I found out that my friend had avoided bringing up several important issues during our initial talks. If he had discussed these considerations with me, I would have chosen the other job offer.

Over the next three months, we laid off approximately 200 of the 240 people on staff, and on the last day of November I lost my job. It's no picnic facing Christmas with an empty bank account. The Christmas season has its own social pressures. I felt emotionally deflated and depressed. The change of losing a job hit me, and I went into survival mode. Panicked and depressed, I had to muster every ounce of energy just to get out of bed in the morning.

**"For God hath not given us the spirit of fear;
but of power, and of love, and of a sound mind."**
2 Timothy 1:7, KJV

My first impulse was to blame my friend. I was the victim of deception. I was angry and bitter, and someone should pay. My bill collectors listened to my "victim of deceit" story. Nevertheless, they were more interested in getting their payment. At least the story sounded and felt good to me. Also, I would have long conversations with other laid-off employees who would join in with their own opinions and advice. "Get a lawyer and file suit," someone said. Amidst these conversations and discussions, my world was getting worse, not better.

Sometimes it's better to take the high road. Blaming the CEO wasn't going to help me move forward. What I really wanted was to get my bills paid and the needs of my family taken care of. I understood I needed to change my attitude and choose a new direction. Therefore, the first decision I made was *not* to make the CEO the villain or to make myself the victim. I went from blaming my circumstances and others to claiming the opportunities before me. I started asking myself what I could have done to avoid this. I focused on what I had learned that would help me in the future. Was this easy? No, it wasn't. However, it was better than staying depressed.

Decide to Change

My decision started my turnaround. When someone asked me what had happened and why I had lost my job, I only indicated that "things just didn't work out." Then I changed the topic and talked about my future. I stopped blaming the CEO, or anyone else for that matter. I decided to go to work on the positive things in order to better my circumstances. Thinking negatively always brings people to a low point.

When we're victims, we give in to our emotions. Our energy is depleted, and we have nothing left to help us turn ourselves around, much less help others. We create a heavy fog around us that makes it difficult to see clearly the possibilities that lay before us. I've heard it said that when a door closes, we sometimes spend so much time staring at it that we miss all the other doors we could have opened.

> "What seems nasty, painful, evil, can become a source of beauty, joy, and strength, if faced with an open mind. Every moment is a golden one for him who has the vision to recognize it as such."
> *Henry Miller*

By avoiding the victim, villain, and helpless stories, I could think clearly and direct my energy into more proactive activities—

like finding a way to take care of my family. The following action points really helped me:

- Putting my energies into developing a proactive plan along with the pros and cons of both sending my résumé out for potential interviews for another job and starting my own business.

- Taking ownership of my situation and not blaming others.

- Looking at my financial situation realistically and prioritizing what had to get paid and what could wait. Even though both had downsides to them, creating a triage was still helpful and realistic.

- Calling my bank and creditors, explaining to them my situation, and asking if I could pay the interest only. In some cases this worked out fine. But not in all cases. What did help was that my creditors seemed to appreciate my proactive approach.

- Reading positive self-help or spiritual books daily. This helped to focus on the good and the opportunities to come, not on the past.

- Thinking about the good things I had instead of thinking how bad my situation was. Things like good health, friends and family that believed in me, an inventory of my own capabilities, etc.

- Creating meetings with my "propeller" friends to help me move forward, stay encouraged, and remain focused on working my plan.

- Stopping any negative self-talk and avoiding the victim, villain, and helpless stories.

Eventually things did work out. Within a few days, I came upon an opportunity to create enough funds to take care of our financial needs for a few months. The opportunity which presented itself was only visible when I was thinking positively. Remaining a victim created a tendency to miss the opportunities. Why? Because the victim role clouded my ability to see new opportunities.

The old adage about "not seeing the forest for the trees" is true. It's hard to see the big picture "forest" when you have a "tree" right in front of you. If seeing opportunity and getting out of the victim mode is challenging to you, then have a trusted friend or advisor help you see your way through the trees. However, the best thing you can do is become a warrior.

Thrivers Focus on Being Warriors

When I was sixteen, my best friend Mark and I worked at a local pizza store. I made and served pizza every Friday and Saturday night from 5:30 PM until 12:00 AM. One evening Mark told me some friends of ours were going to be camping and riding their dirt bikes at the lake and suggested we go after work and spend the night. I called my dad and got permission. My father often took me and my siblings camping to the same lake, so he knew where we were going to be. After we closed the store, Mark told me the other news he omitted when he suggested we go to the lake. He had invited four other friends to go with us. All of them were girls who worked at the pizza place. It seemed the girls had cooked up a good story and told their parents they were spending the night at each other's houses. I was a shy kid, especially around girls I didn't know very well, so I wasn't excited about the idea at all.

The lake was about an hour's drive, which wouldn't have been too bad, except that Mark's old 1965 Rambler didn't have a passenger side seat. He had been working on his older-than-dirt car and had taken the front seat out. Three of the girls sat in the back seat, and the other girl and I sat on the floor next to the driver's seat. I was somewhat upset that Mark had planned the whole thing, but I made do. The girls, all fifteen to sixteen years old, laughed, giggled, and told stories about their boyfriends all the way to the lake. We finally arrived at the lake around 3:00 AM. The night was pitch-black; no moon or stars were out. We were driving down unlit country roads looking for our friends. Mark had the driver side window down and was trying to remember exactly how to get there.

I was somewhat sleepy by this point and lay down on a quilt where the passenger seat should have been. The girl that was sitting with me had fallen asleep too and was lying on my shoulder. I didn't mind at all and was feeling better about Mark bringing these girls after all. As I was starting to fall asleep, Mark looked in his review mirror and said that there were police cars with their lights flashing in the distance. I remember Mark telling me there must be a robbery or fire going on, because there were at least seven police cars coming our way.

We decided to pull over so they could pass. Suddenly, like a scene out of an FBI movie, we were surrounded by white, blue, and red lights and the sound of tires screeching to a halt. With all the tires screeching, the doors slamming, and the cops yelling, I couldn't help but think that someone was in big trouble. While lying down with a girl in my arms, I was covering my eyes to hide from the number of flashlights in my face. At that time, I realized *we* were in very big trouble. There was a cop on a loud speaker yelling at the people surrounding the car to back away. It wasn't the cops looking through the window down on me, but the anxious dads of these girls! Like Alfalfa in a *Little Rascals* movie, my hair stood straight up and my eyes were as big as glazed donuts. I knew I was in serious trouble.

Then out of the darkness came a voice that sounded like God Himself. It was my own dad, taking command and ordering the other fathers to get back in their cars. Even the police didn't argue with him. My father opened the door and ushered every girl to her parents. When he was finished, he got in the backseat and commanded Mark to drive us home. After a few minutes of silence, my dad calmly asked what had been going on. I apologized to Mark and then spilled the beans.

My dad said he had received a call from the police about the situation and knew he had better come along. "Those dads were as angry as hornets ... I am sure both of you boys could have gotten hurt," my dad said. After a while the situation turned into a comic relief. We were all laughing so hard that I cried. I don't think I was more proud of my dad in my whole life than at that moment. My dad was a warrior, and my hero, who had saved us from some very angry people.

When you think of a warrior, what image comes to mind? For me, it's the movie *Gladiator* with Russell Crowe, or *The Patriot* with Mel Gibson. In the movies, you get it all—blood, bullets, bayonets, bullies, and battle scenes, with a little history mixed in. Warriors in Hollywood are somewhat misleading, though. We're left with the impression that the handsome guy with the cocky smile and the reckless attitude (who dodges bullets and gets the girl while always sporting perfect hair) is what makes a good warrior. Not so!

The real warriors are real people—men and women—dealing with real issues. All have one thing in common: the courage to face life head-on.

Slaying the Giant Takes Courage

Warriors are Thrivers! I am reminded of a Sunday school story about a young shepherd boy named David who takes on a giant named Goliath. This giant stood almost ten feet tall. He had a 125-pound coat of armor, a 17-pound spear, and a 16-pound spearhead. Goliath was so powerful that 40,000 soldiers chose not to answer his invitation to fight him alone.

As a young boy, David's job was to feed and protect his father's sheep. Twice while on his watch, the sheep were attacked by a wild animal. Both times David tracked down the beast, took the sheep out of its mouth, and killed the beast with his bare hands. Was David afraid? Sure he was. But he faced his greatest fear with courage.

So when Goliath the giant issued his challenge, this young shepherd boy knew that he could face him and take him down. Using the only resources he had, David initiated the attack, shocking everyone—Goliath included! The giant died after David hit him between the eyes with a rock.

David had the three primary traits of a warrior. He:

1. Had the right cause and purpose in his heart.
2. Had the experience of victory in the past that gave him the experience to look forward.
3. Didn't complain about what he didn't have, but did the impossible with what he did have.

Known as a virtue, courage has at least two components: a feeling of fear and a perceived external danger. In this example, David exercised courage to face his fear. Courage is a decision.

A warrior is someone who exercises courage in the face of fear and perceived danger and engages in the battle aggressively or energetically. We see this every day—people who are hit hard with the difficult circumstances in life and yet still choose to face their fears and move, undeterred, toward their goals.

> **"Courage is doing what you're afraid to do.
> There can be no courage unless you're scared."**
> *Eddie Rickenbacker*

Warriors Make War

Do you have giants that you are confronting? Maybe you have lost a job and fear getting a new one. Maybe you are facing a relationship meltdown and fear the loss. Maybe you are a single mom or dad dealing with fear of the future. Do you feel stuck in survival mode? Then it's time for you to become a warrior. Warriors face their giants head on. They make war.

Making war is intentional and requires planning and execution. Are you putting all your energy into fighting the giants in your life, or are you burning brain cells and energy on surviving victim roles? While warriors make war, victims make drama. When you are in warrior mode, you spend time thinking about what you can do to help your situation. You are planning, thinking ahead, meeting with propeller friends, avoiding helpless stories, and discovering your options. Victims complain about what they lack and the resources they do not have. They tend to spend their time talking too much about the past and not enough about the future. The giants in their life seem to be the topic of most of their conversations.

Consider Lois Ferrara, an example of a warrior who is taking what life has thrown at her and fighting back. In the span of two decades, her doctors diagnosed her with Hodgkin's disease, then lymphatic, thyroid, breast, and lung cancer. Mrs. Ferrara has endured more than a dozen surgeries and countless medical treatments and has emerged cancer-free every time. She is currently training for the Breast Cancer Three-Day Walk. She is also using her experiences to counsel those who have been diagnosed with cancer or are recovering, helping them through the process. Friends and doctors of Mrs. Ferrara credit her "Can-do" attitude as one of the major factors in her ability to do more than just survive. She is using humor to encourage herself and others not to give up. She also stays focused on the positive side of life. Instead of thinking about her mortality, she is busy doing other things. She bakes cupcakes and delivers them to retirement homes. The local fire department is another one of her common recipients.

Lois isn't making drama for herself and others. Instead, she is fighting back by exercising courage instead of fear. She is a modern day warrior who has found a reason to fight back.

Warriors also fight the battles of life for a cause and a purpose. While visiting a war memorial, I was drawn into the stories of soldiers who had died in battle. One story was about a young man who threw himself on top of a grenade. He lost his life but saved the lives of others. I guess he didn't have much time to think about what he was doing, but there was a reason he threw himself on the grenade. The reason—his cause—was his love for and the protection of his buddies! Warriors in life fight back because what they love, or whom they love, is at risk. They fight to get back what their troubles have taken away.

To move from surviving to thriving, we need to know our cause and our purpose. For me, it's my kids. I want them to be proud of their dad, and I want to give them a promising future. My purpose is to thrive for myself and my kids.

What is so valuable or important to you that you would aggressively make war for it? If we are going to fight the giants in our lives, then we need to recognize and face another giant: Fear.

> **"A ship in harbor is safe, but that is not what ships are built for."**
> *John A. Shedd*

Dealing with the Giant Called Fear

Ann Landers, the well-known newspaper columnist, received an average of ten thousand letters a month. Almost all of them were from people burdened with life's problems. She was asked if there was one problem that people seemed to struggle with more than any other. Her reply? Fear!

Fear is a common problem from which none of us is immune. Many doctors would agree that succumbing to chronic fear can literally make us sick.

If you're going to move beyond surviving to a thriving warrior life, then you will need to face your greatest enemy, and that's fear. There are two types of fear I find in my life: real fear and false fear. Most of us have experienced real fear. Slamming on the brakes to avoid a collision creates real fear. Waking up at night to find a stranger in your room creates real fear. Watching buildings collapse after a terrorist attack creates real fear. Real fear is a natural, protective response to danger.

Business owners also struggle with this giant in many forms: a fear of poverty, a fear of criticism, a fear of rejection, or a fear of failing. Most of us have fears that relate to a fear of growing old, a fear of illness, a fear of being separated from loved ones, and a fear of death.

We all struggle with another type of fear that is dangerous in its own way. This is known as false fear. Here is an acronym that is helpful to understanding what false fear is all about:

False Evidence Appearing Real = **FEAR**

False fear appears real to us in some way, but it is an illusion. We create so much of our own pain and anxiety with our false fears. I have found that most of the things I worry about don't happen anyway. However, these false fears still have a way of keeping me up at night.

My associate Suzi tells her experience of growing up as an "Air Force brat." Her family moved many times to different countries and locations, which in turn required that she receive more medical shots than those who live in one place their entire lives. As a result, Suzi developed a huge fear of needles that stayed with her long into adulthood. She particularly recalls having to get blood drawn when she was sixteen. She was so fearful of getting a needle stuck in her that she didn't sleep at all the night before. When the nurse came in the next day, Suzi panicked, gave in to her fears, and ran down the hall away from the needle and the nurse.

Recently, Suzi experienced back problems that required several spinal injections and IVs. She said she was so tired of fighting the pain that she was willing to let them do anything. When they did the first IV, Suzi discovered something very interesting. The pain was minimal! The needles were nothing compared to the anxiety and anguish caused by *the fear of the needle*. Suzi's fear of the needle was larger than the reality of the actual pain.

"Don't be afraid to take a big step. You can't cross a chasm in two jumps."
David Lloyd George

False fears also affect and damage our relationships. For instance, if you're afraid that your child will grow up to be a drug addict, you may try to control every minute of his or her life. You won't give them any breathing room to make mistakes. You try to ban them from activities that could possibly expose them to an evil world. Yet what your child doesn't receive is your trust and the freedom to make decisions on his or her own. In return, he or she could be doing just the opposite of what you would have your child do.

I have a friend who was raised by a father who was extremely racial toward certain ethnic groups. She eventually took an interest in a young Hispanic man that her dad disapproved of. In the end, she got pregnant. I asked her why she made that decision. She told me her father was so paranoid and controlling over her seeing Hispanic boys that it made her angry. When I asked why she was angry, she confided that she really wanted her father to just trust her and not make such an issue over it. Today she has a healthy, beautiful boy. However, her father still doesn't want to have anything to do with her or his grandson.

Why was this father so controlling? What was his fear? I believe that he was consumed by the fear of having his daughter marry the wrong person. His fear controlled his behavior. His controlling behavior provoked his daughter to date the very person he feared. I find this interesting and often wonder in my own life if I am doing things because of false fear. We sometimes try very hard to make sure our fears do not happen only to find in the end we predicted our own demise.

False fear can cause my own children to:

- Wear clothes I don't want them to wear.
- Listen to music I don't want them to hear.
- Date the person I don't want them to see.
- Seek the drugs I don't want them to touch.

For instance, one of my children wanted to play football. Like me, he was very thin and small in his early teens. When he asked if he could play football, my immediate answer was that he could not play. I gave him a few reasons like "You are already involved in too many things" and "I don't have the time in my schedule to drive you everywhere." Honestly, my reason for him not to play football was because I was fearful he would get hurt. Could he get hurt? Yes. However, my fear of him getting hurt motivated me to prevent him from playing altogether.

Another example is when I wanted to go to a conference that would benefit me professionally. My spouse at the time agreed that the conference would be helpful. As the day approached for me to leave for the conference, however, my spouse became more critical and cynical about my going. Some of our discussions about my going were so frustrating that I would have to leave the room and end the discussion. In the end, the real reason for my spouse's negative attitude was because she had heard from her friends that many men have affairs while at business conferences. This was a very powerful fear for her that changed her behavior to irrational and controlling and also caused me to become angry at her. This not only created more stress on the relationship but also something even more hurtful: her false fear created an absence of trust.

False fear creates distrust, and with distrust comes a desire to control and a restriction of freedom. Trust is a core ingredient in healthy relationships. I have found that giving in to false fear doesn't breed trust. It breeds distrust, disharmony, and, eventually, rebellion.

Warriors who maintain a thriving life understand that they need to be aware of these false fears. Why? Because false fears anchor you to the giants in your life.

Remember that false fear is destructive to your ability to create the life you want. The steps from Survivor to Thriver (Victim to

Warrior) are to exercise courage, face the challenges head on, and be aware of the giant called Fear.

> **"Fear is only as deep as the mind allows."**
> *Japanese proverb*

Summary

In this chapter, we looked at the difference between surviving and thriving as it relates to the picture of a victim and warrior. Review the chart below and look at the characteristics. Where do you see yourself? Imagine having coffee with a trusted friend, someone who would tell you the truth about what he or she sees in you. Would this friend say that you are in a victim role or a warrior role? Come up with examples of each behavior in your own life to discover where you need to make adjustments.

Surviving		*Thriving*
Victim	**vs.**	**Warrior**
- Blaming		- Accountable
- Hopeless		- Determined
- Emotional		- Logical

In the next chapter, we will take a look at another powerful key difference between those who just survive and those who thrive. This stage is where many people discover core breakthroughs. Understanding the difference between becoming a parasite or a player will be one of the determining factors to go beyond just surviving or choosing to pick up the baseball bat and risk taking a few more swings at life. In the next chapter, we will find out what it takes to get back into the game.

Insight

Victim Versus Warrior

The first step in moving from victim to warrior is to think about the differences between these questions:

"Why did this happen to me?" (victim)

versus

"What could I have done to avoid this?" (warrior)

"Why do bad things always happen to me?" (victim)

versus

"What did I do to contribute to this problem?" (warrior)

Remember the five Ws from school? Who, What, Where, When, and Why? And the sixth question, How? Generally, the best questions begin with What and How. Questions that begin with one of these two words tend to be productive questions that call for a sense of responsibility and ownership.

Ask yourself: Do I ask victim questions or warrior questions?

As I process an adverse situation, do my questions begin with "Why," or do they begin with "What" and "How"?

Am I acting like a victim or a warrior?

Chapter Six

Parasite Versus Player

A parasite is an organism that grows, feeds, and is sheltered on or in a different organism while contributing nothing to the survival of its host. In human relationships, a parasite is a metaphor for a person who habitually takes advantage of the generosity of others without making any useful return, draining the life out of everyone around them.

In 2005, when Hurricane Katrina devastated New Orleans, survivors were sent to shelters as close as Texas and Louisiana, and as far away as New York. These people needed shelter, food, clothing, and encouragement. Good-natured Americans came to the rescue of their brothers and sisters. Millions of dollars in aid were raised. However, after a while, I began hearing reports of Katrina survivors who were not interested in actively helping themselves or moving on. Many started complaining because their expectations were not met. The Red Cross didn't get the money out fast enough, or the president didn't respond quickly enough. Some of the victims were even complaining about the help they were receiving. I began wondering what they were doing to help their situation. Did they think everybody else should carry their burden? I'm not being insensitive to their needs. However, some survivors in certain circumstances have a tendency to act more like parasites. They can attach themselves to the services of others or feed off of the emotions of others without giving anything back.

Same Old Story Over and Over

Have you ever had a conversation with someone who just loves to tell you about all the bad things that are happening in his or her life? Years later, these individuals are still telling the same old story, over and over. At this stage, parasites are not interested in your advice or counsel. They are interested only in what *you* can do to make their life better. Their goal is for you to buy into their story and encourage them with your sympathy. They feel they deserve help from others. And they can spend their energy creating a laundry list of excuses as to why they can't take any action.

Complaining is a key characteristic of parasites. Complainers like to express feelings of pain, dissatisfaction, or resentment. So when we complain, we tend to attract complainers like ourselves. Suddenly, we're surrounded by complainers. Doing well in college was important to me because I paid for my own education. Studying and making acceptable grades was hard work. I did not develop good study habits in high school, so reading a single chapter in a book took me a long time. When it came time to test for a subject like math or history, I did the best I could. Often when the test scores came out, I received an average grade, and sometimes my grade was worse than the average. To make myself feel better, I would share my low scores with other classmates. It made me feel better to find someone whose scores equaled mine or were worse.

In one instance, I found I was consistently complaining about a particular class in which I had not done well. For weeks, I would bring up my low scores and complain about how hard the class was, how bad the professor taught the class, and how everybody else was failing, too. After a while, I remember one of my study buddies pulled me aside and said he was tired of hearing how my low score was everybody else's problem. At first, he made me angry and upset. However, after I thought about it, I was glad he confronted me because I needed to do more than survive a college class. I needed to go beyond surviving and into a more thriving mode. I took my friend's advice and stopped complaining.

Afterward, I became very sensitive to my complaining and whining about poor test scores. I stopped using my friends as a way to gain support for my shortcomings. I found that when I wasn't complaining to someone about my situation, my mind was free to discover other possibilities and solutions. For instance, I learned to start reading chapters before the class professor covered them. This helped me to learn the information twice. I also discovered that there was a certain time during the day that was better for studying than others; at this time my energy level was higher. I picked up a book on memorizing material that helped, too. Focusing on these opportunities and changes also helped my negative attitude.

Why Parasites Like to Complain

There are many reasons parasites like to complain. Sometimes they complain because they simply want someone to know that they are suffering. Once they can find someone to hear their story, they feel a little satisfied. But this satisfaction is only short term. Soon parasites are off to find another host that will listen to their story. Currently, I have a business associate who is going through a divorce. Every time we get together or speak on the phone, the conversation turns toward talking about his break-up and his opinion of it. It is healthy to talk it through. However, most of the conversation is simply him complaining. For me, listening to someone complain about the same thing every time we meet is emotionally draining. Now I am finding I avoid his phone calls.

> **"When you blame others, you give up your power to change."**
> *Dr. Robert Anthony*

At other times, parasites may repeatedly complain about their troubles out of self-pity or the desire to gain sympathy. Others may show they understand, but no matter what they say or do for these parasites, the parasites are dissatisfied and continue to complain.

Parasites may complain because they want someone who will fix their problem. Instead of asking someone directly for help, parasites repeatedly recount their sad story in the hopes that the listener will get the message and change the situation. Parasites may do this because they are too frightened or lazy to try to solve the problem themselves. For instance, a parasite might complain to a work colleague about a challenging situation at the office, hoping that this colleague will go to the manager about it. Alternatively, he or she might call the friends and family of his lover or spouse and complain about their relationship with hopes that the family members will support his or her cause.

Another reason parasites complain is to vent their emotions and their feeling of powerlessness. They become critical of relationships around them; they target those who hurt them or people who caused their pain in life. Parasites feel powerless to change their situation, so they create "distortion campaigns" to prosecute, convict, and banish what they perceive as the hurtful people and events around them.

Parasites can also complain simply to hear themselves talk; sometimes they don't really want to resolve their difficulties and just enjoy telling the story many times to various people. They are stuck in a complaining rut of their own making.

How do you help parasites out of this rut? You might ask these complainers a few questions in order to help them. For example, "What ideas do you have for what can be done?" or "What ideas do you have that could help in this situation?" These questions prompt them to refocus on getting out of the survivor-parasite mode. Instead of allowing them to get lost in their stories, prod them to see that they could change their view of the situation or their behavior and become a Thriver. Instead of a parasite, they can become a player.

Thrivers Strive to Be Players

Unlike parasites who sit on the sidelines and whine about losing, players get into the game and do their part to win. Players choose to step up to the plate and swing the bat. If they miss the ball, they keep at it until they eventually connect.

Remember the movie *The Natural* starring Robert Redford? In this story, an unknown, middle-aged player with a mysterious past named Roy Hobbs appears out of nowhere to take a losing 1930s baseball team to the top of the league standings. With the aid of a bat cut from a tree that was struck by lightning, Hobbs lives out the fame he should have had earlier in his life; as a young man he was inexplicably shot by a woman, which cut short his dreams of playing baseball. After a number of years, we see middle-aged Hobbs re-entering the world of baseball. I imagine that during the years he was out of the game, a character like Hobbs likely spent many days complaining about his situation, recounting the events over and over in his mind. We don't know how he recovered or at what point he decided to return because the story doesn't give us the details. Nevertheless, I imagine that one day Hobbs got tired of being a Survivor and a parasite. That was the day he chose to get back into the game and become a player.

Players Will Discuss, Not Complain

Unlike parasites that tend to complain about their issues, players understand the difference between complaining and discussing issues. Complaining focuses on the emotions, the hurt or loss others have caused them, and the "unfairness" of the situation. When discussing an issue, it's best to focus on the facts as they actually happened. Try to understand the origin or root cause of the problem and discuss a possible solution. A key difference is in our attitude and motivation for bringing an issue to the surface. Having a discussion in a proactive, constructive way keeps the responsibility for the problem where it needs to be and helps avoid blaming others when the situation cannot be controlled.

Discussing issues without complaining about them helps us get back into the game of life. Complaining will keep us stuck where we are. If help is needed, we should ask for it directly instead of whining over and over with the hopes that someone will rescue us or feel sorry for us. Discussing problems and issues draws people to us and allows others to open up, too. This opens the door for constructive communication about the situation. Financial hardships, a friendship gone wrong, an unfair policy at the office, a spouse's uncooperative attitude, the problems of society, the misconceptions of political leaders, or the dishonesty of CEOs— all of these things can be discussed rationally without complaining about them. Players understand that this approach is far more helpful and productive because discussion with knowledgeable people can help give us a new perspective on the situation, which in turn helps us deal with it more effectively.

Accepting the Risk

Is there a risk in choosing to change from a parasite to a player? Absolutely! There is always an element of risk involved, and risk involves loss or hurt, as well as a profit or gain. Will you get hurt again? Yes, you could. However, you could also experience great satisfaction and joy.

I had a dream of starting my own business before I was thirty years old when I began my mini-blind company. I followed that dream, and I was sure it would work. After several years of hard work and sweat, the business failed. I also got hurt. Things just didn't work out as planned. The promises I made to others just didn't happen. Many friends and colleagues were disappointed. I took a risk and suffered losses. At first, I succumbed to parasite-behavior, constantly complaining about what had happened. I would dream about when I would enter the game again and start another company, but it was all just talk. I was wishing for it, hoping for it, longing for it—but nothing happened until I found the courage to be a player again and accept that there are risks.

To be a player, you have to accept the risks, as well as the pain that is part of life's journey. While on the field, football players practice hitting each other. Even with all the padding and equipment, the impact of a three-hundred-pound linebacker will rattle anyone's teeth. Still, for the love of the game, the players take risks.

Players Have Mental Fitness

Players develop a mental discipline to stay focused on their goals and dreams. They don't let others' negative comments, critiques, or opinions get them off track. They understand how important it is to have a strong mental focus. An e-mail story going around about the Tiny Frog Competition (author unknown) illustrates this point beautifully.

Once upon a time there was a bunch of tiny frogs who arranged a running competition among themselves. The goal was to reach the top of a very high tower. A huge crowd gathered around the tower to see the race and cheer on the contestants. The race began.

No one in the crowd really believed that the tiny frogs would reach the top of the tower. "Oh, it's way too difficult!!" "They will never make it to the top." "Not a chance that they will succeed. The tower is too high!"

The tiny frogs began collapsing, one by one—except for those who, in a fresh tempo, were climbing higher and higher.

The crowd continued to yell, "It is too difficult. No one will make it!"

More tiny frogs got tired and gave up. But one continued higher and higher and higher. At the end, everyone else had given up climbing the tower except for one tiny frog who, after a big effort, was the only one who reached the top!

All of the other tiny frogs naturally wanted to know how this one frog managed to do it. A contestant asked the winner how he had found the strength to succeed and reach the goal.

The winner couldn't answer because he couldn't hear the question. He was deaf!

Players Demonstrate Spiritual Fitness

The kids on my street when I was seven years old spent most evenings playing games. "Red Rover, Red Rover" was a game we liked to play, as well as cops and robbers. Flag football was a favorite, too. I remember Johnny, one of my best friends, would not only initiate these activities, but if the game wasn't going in his favor, Johnny would change or add to the rules. This frustrated me because Johnny would change the rules to meet his need to win. In the same way, the motivation to pick yourself up, dust yourself off, and start all over seems to be grounded in something deeper than ourselves. Personally, I think it's a spiritual connection. This is why I believe thriving players have something inside of them that motivates their soul to head forward with great determination. Something I term "spiritual fitness."

Spiritual fitness is equally important in a player mindset. Beliefs are the foundation on which we live our lives—beliefs that help us answer the deeper questions like *Who am I? Why am I here? What is my purpose?* These are the key questions we ask when life gets us down.

What we believe is critical to moving from surviving to thriving. Personally, I believe in a higher power—I'm sure I am guided by something greater than myself. My personal spirituality also includes following the teachings of the Bible. This is a book that I trust completely. Not because it is still the most published book in the world, but because it speaks to my heart about the things that are important to me. It answers questions like:

- Is there an afterlife or heaven?
- How can I know where I am going when I die?
- What is my purpose in life?
- Who created the universe and world around me?
- Why do we have pain and suffering?
- What is the best way to live?
- Does God love me?

This kind of foundation is important to me and gives me a compass to guide me through rough waters. When life gets difficult and the storms are fierce, it's comforting to know there is a lighthouse ahead that gives clarity and direction to avoid the reefs. Thrivers understand that in order to be a player in life, there has to be someone in control. Someone who understands life's games and has a right way or wrong way to live life. Imagine having my friend Johnny as your spiritual guide. The rules would be constantly changing. Without a solid spiritual compass, you will be lost.

Otherwise, what's the purpose? Who makes the rules? Are there absolutes that can be trusted? Or is our ultimate destiny nothing more than the hope of just getting the next birthday? Even that is depressing! For me, the spiritual compass is the Bible whose author claims to be God. I can stand on these unchanging principles when the world around me is constantly changing.

For others it's something else. Nevertheless, our belief systems are foundational to our desire to move ahead.

Players Make the Call

Players don't wait for someone else to make things happen. They take the necessary action to make decisions instead of waiting for something or someone else to do it for them.

Consider Tina, a newly divorced mom, who didn't have a clue as to how she was going to support her family. Her ex-husband was not paying any child support. Her choice was to complain about it or direct her energies and attention to making a living. After twenty-one years of marriage, she found herself facing the reality of being solely responsible for paying the bills. She was terrified, as most people would have been.

As a teenager she had a love for dancing, and she taught dance classes until she went to college and then married. One day while thinking about what she could do, a new idea sparked. She could get back into teaching dance lessons in the town where she currently lived. She decided to place an ad in the local paper promoting a new dance class. This was a big risk for Tina because, among other things, the town she lived in was a small farming community. To her surprise, seventy people showed up for her first class! Today she has been recertified as a dance instructor, and her new business is doing very well. Tina initiated an idea. Instead of complaining, she came up with a solution and drew upon her knowledge and skill. As a player, Tina decided to move forward and make the call.

When my family moved to a new town in East Texas, we were anxious to build new relationships. We joined a new church and were eager to get to know the other members. After two months at the church, I still didn't know anybody very well and was feeling frustrated. One day on the phone, I mentioned to a long-time friend of mine how unfriendly this church was. "Nobody wants to get to know us," I said. I was complaining about the situation but not discussing the situation for possible solutions. Thankfully, my friend directed me to take the initiative and invite people over to the house after church. If starting new friendships was important to me, then why was I waiting for someone to get to know me? Why was I waiting for the friendships to develop on their own?

The next week I told my family, "We're going to have people over after church this Sunday. We'll make beans and rice and cornbread and invite about five or six couples." Beans and cornbread is an easy meal to prepare and was also within our budget at the time. I was hoping people were more interested in getting together than they were in getting a gourmet meal!

After church, I went from person to person and asked them if they would like to come to lunch. It didn't take long until we had a group of friends-in-the-making coming over. What started out as complaining changed into becoming a player by making the call to invite people over for lunch. The results were wonderful! Many of the people we invited had the same desire to meet new people and were as hungry for friendships as we were. I was so glad that my family and I had made the call.

Players Have a Kemosabe

One of my favorite childhood shows was *The Lone Ranger*. This was a long-running early radio and television show about a masked cowboy in the American Old West who gallops about righting injustices, usually with the aid of a clever American Indian called Tonto and his horse Silver.

Tonto always greeted the Lone Ranger by saying, "Kemosabe." The origin of this expression is somewhat unclear, but James Jewell (an early director of the radio series) said the name originated from a boy's camp located on Mullett Lake, Michigan, that his father-in-law directed from 1911 to 1941. The translation meant "trusty scout," which Tonto explains in the pilot of the Clayton Moore TV series, *Enter the Lone Ranger*. Fran Striker, the writer of *The Lone Ranger* scripts, also said the actual expression was Ta-i ke-mo sah-bee, which he said meant "Greetings, trusty scout."

Over time, the phrase "faithful friend" has also been associated with the term Kemosabe. The Lone Ranger was the person Tonto looked to as the one who knew the answers to difficult situations. As a kid, I remember how Tonto and the Lone Ranger would get out of some very difficult circumstances with a good attitude and quick problem-solving skills. (Of course, unlike the Lone Ranger, my real-life problems take longer than a thirty-minute TV show to solve.) To jump from a parasite Survivor to a thriving player, you need to look around you and determine your Kemosabes.

Who are the trusted friends that you turn to when you need to discuss life's situations and challenges? Who are the people with whom you can trust to share your heart, knowing that they will hold your confidence? Who are the Kemosabes that listen to your issues without making judgments? Players looking to thrive know they need Kemosabes in their life because these are the people who give them insight and wisdom as well as encouragement when they need it. I have been so fortunate in my life to have had some wonderful Kemosabes. People like Pastor Kim Beckham, Pastor Richard Spencer, my brother Pastor Rick Sydnor, and my staff at my office.

Summary

In this chapter, we have evaluated the difference between thriving as a player or surviving in a parasite role. Once again, it is normal when struggling through life's challenging moments to become more passive, allowing others to help us. We need to gain energy from others because we have little left. We need the attention and support from our family and friends. However, at some point your friends, family, and even you need to move to a more thriving role and become more assertive. You must begin producing energy for yourself and others as well as proactively making plans and visualizing the future. Spending time thinking about the chart below can help you identify the areas where change is most needed. Take time to write down your thoughts. Where do you fit? What mode do you see yourself in? Then find someone you feel safe with and share what you wrote down.

Surviving		*Thriving*
Parasite	vs.	**Player**
- Passive		- Assertive
- Energy-absorbing		- Energy-producing
- Reactive		- Proactive

Being in charge and in control of your life is critical to taking the life you have and creating the life you want. In the next chapter, we will look at one more pair of contrasting behaviors. Understanding these two characteristics will become a launching point for your career, marriage, business, and future relationships. We will discover how Survivors tend to be more like actors on stage while Thrivers reflect the characteristics of a director. Directors are writing the story of their lives as well as creating the production. Some of the descriptions will surprise you as you discover which role you are currently playing. To reach beyond just surviving your circumstances, you need to discover if you are just acting or if you are directing.

Insight

Parasite Versus Player

Ask yourself these questions:

- How much of my conversation is in the form of complaints?
- Do I always have an excuse when things go wrong?
- Are those around me negative or positive?
- Who are my trusted friends?
- Do I have a mental and spiritual focus?
- Am I taking the initiative to create a better life?
- What steps can I take to "make the call" instead of waiting for something to happen?

Chapter Seven

Actor Versus Director

I recently made a trip to New York for a business meeting. I decided to take my daughter, who had always dreamed of going to New York and seeing a Broadway show. While she and I were standing in line for discount tickets, we decided upon a show called *The Spelling Bee*. We didn't know anything about it, but we decided to give it a try. I have to say that the show was worth every penny. The actors were very funny, they were engaging with the audience, their characters were very believable, their timing was perfect, they delivered their lines loud and clear, and they were really professional.

However, while watching the play I also noticed a strong contrast between the actors and the director. I began thinking about how these two positions are similar to the surviving or thriving mentality.

Actor or Director in Life?

In the play, the actors were the ones that we could physically see and watch onstage. However, the director is behind the scenes and only mentioned in the show program. It was the actors who bowed at the end of the show and received the applause from a grateful audience. The director, however, received his or her glory from how the audience responded to the show from the opening scene to the last applause. I found this interesting because although the actors portrayed the characters on stage, they were also performing under the direction of the director. The director has the vision of the play as well as the power of selecting the right actors and stage hands and is ultimately responsible for the whole production. In the end, it's the actors who are on stage, but the director who is ultimately in control.

When we are in survival mode, in many ways we are like the actors on stage responding to cues. When we decide to move to a more thriving life, we make a significant change and become the directors in our lives.

An actor is someone who works in a play or movie that portrays a different character and acts out a part in front of an audience. Their performance involves memorizing lines, calling up emotions, and knowing the proper time to deliver the material. When we are in survival mode, we have a tendency to become actors. Actors in survival mode need direction from something outside of themselves. Often they can be waiting on someone else to show them their part. They need someone to give them direction and focus. I have found in my own life that I tend to be an actor at times when I don't feel very confident. That's when I look for others to give me feedback, direction, or their opinion.

When Being an Actor Is Necessary

For example, when I was in counseling for my divorce, they advised me not to consider remarriage until after three years. And because I had been married twenty years or more, I was advised to consider a five-year wait before remarriage. The advice I received also suggested that if I had teenagers, I should wait until they graduated from high school. In the end, the total was about ten years before I should remarry. My first thought was, "I'm not going to do that because it sounds unreasonable to me!" When I questioned it, my counselor explained the reasoning behind it.

Basically, the counselor said that it takes time to recover and sort through the current situation. Time helps to reconcile the feelings and reasons for the divorce, and time was a key factor in healing. The counselor also noted that each person is different; however, on average, it can take anywhere from three to four years to work through the process in order to make a healthy decision about a future marriage. One of the reasons my counselor suggested this course of action was that personal trauma leaves us with a high level of emotion and unresolved hurt. If we don't take the time to heal, then we could create the opportunity for more pain through poor decisions made by not listening to wise advice.

Honestly, I didn't like this advice. However, I was currently surviving a difficult change in my life. Having a counselor who could give me direction was helpful. I didn't understand completely why I should wait at least three years before making a decision as serious as marriage, but I did understand that I should give myself time. I appreciated the advice because at that point in my life I needed direction.

In the same way, there are times in our lives when taking on the role of an "actor" is necessary—we must listen to and heed the advice of others who are wiser and more experienced. I'm not saying that acting is a bad thing. At times we need the direction of others.

Actor and Survival Behavior

Regardless of the fact that sometimes the actor role is necessary, there are some negative aspects of being an actor—especially when we cling to the actor role too long and refuse to become the directors of our lives. Survivors behave like actors when they:

- **Take direction from outside, not inside.** When actors are playing a role, they need someone else to give them feedback. Actors may think they are saying the right lines with the right body language, but it's not until the director helps them work through the right movements that they begin to see their character develop. When we are in survival mode, we tend not to see what course our decisions could take. Just like actors who need coaching on these decisions to be sure they are seeing things clearly, there are times when we need direction and help from others who see the facts and realities which we may not see. Again, it's not bad to take direction from others when you are surviving a crisis. However, transitioning into a more thriving life requires you to become the director.

- **Live for the applause of others.** Actors live for the attention of others. The attention and sympathy we get from others who hear our Survivor stories is addictive. Giving in to the desire to talk about our past hurts too much and receiving others' attention can take hold of us and own us, much like a drug addiction. If we are not careful, we can relive the past in order to feed that addictive need for attention. This thirst for sympathy and attention could keep us stuck in survival mode.

- **Act like someone else.** Actors on stage assume the personality of the character they are pretending to be—the person they want you to see. However, you don't really get to know the real person inside. Survivor-actors tend not to be transparent and open. When in survival mode, our emotions

96

about the situation can run so high that we are not sure who we are. We are unsure about our decisions, and we tend to second-guess whatever we do decide. I have seen this many times in the assessments we give professionals for their personal development. Sometimes when their assessment reports come in, their behavioral scores are skewed or do not seem normal. This is often because at the moment they took the assessment, they were suffering from some kind of trauma such as divorce, the loss of a child or a parent, financial pressures, uncertainty about their current job, or extreme work pressures. These skewed scores indicate that the person isn't sure who he or she is and, therefore, cannot answer the questions consistently. Oftentimes, they are trying to be all things to all people.

- **Base their confidence on what others think of them.** All of us struggle with rejection at some level. However, moving forward into a more thriving mode means that you may need to stand alone with your decision, and that's OK. You know you are transitioning from survivor to thriver mode when you feel confident about your decisions and can stand behind them. Actors will base how they feel about themselves from the comments and opinions of others. They place more value on what others think than what they think. For example, I know a pastor who is in constant turmoil because of the comments spoken—or unspoken—from influential people in the church. He fears his congregation will be unhappy with his performance. Like an actor waiting for audience applause, he weighs his decisions according to what church members will think, not on what he believes is right.

- **Act on cue:** Just as "Lights, camera, action" is a key command from the director on a movie set, we could be waiting for our cue to act or move toward some kind of action or for someone to tell us what to do. Actors will perform on cue when given direction. Often in survival mode, we are waiting on direction from someone else because we are not sure we can trust our own decisions.

> **"Letting go of expectations gives us the energy to live spontaneously and joyously, for each moment holds its magic, even when the moment is painful."**
> *Will Limon*

In contrast to actors, Thrivers are more apt to take charge and direct their own lives. Let's take a look at what this means when we practice this approach.

Thrivers Direct Their Lives

In the midst of trying to tread water and stay afloat after the fiasco with my mini-blind business, my creditors began calling non-stop, asking when they would be paid. My answer was, "When I get paid, you get paid." I started avoiding them altogether. Debt was an embarrassment and humiliation that only strengthened the message that I had failed. Wishing that the calls would go away, I instructed employees to answer the creditors' calls by saying, "Stepp's not here. Can I take a message?" even when I was in the office.

Customers who had placed orders and paid a deposit were told that their orders were lost or delayed in shipment, when the fact was I didn't have the money to pay my vendors. Every day was a nightmare as I tried to balance presenting a business that was doing well in order to keep our customers and knowing that the doors would be closing at any time. With poor cash flow, slow market activity for our product, debt piling to the sky, and employees jumping ship, my options seemed limited. I felt like an actor on stage just waiting for someone to give me my next line. The applause from the audience was dying, and so was I.

I felt depressed and guilty for lying to customers about their orders. One day while in the midst of this current storm, I asked myself, "Who's in control here: the creditors or me?" This was not a play, and I was not on stage. This was real life, and I had real problems. I decided that I needed to jump into a more thriving mode by taking the director role and moving out of the surviving actor role.

I remember asking myself what I had control over. I had control over my response to the situation. I also had control over what I did or did not say. I knew I was not being truthful to myself or to others. What I needed to do was just deal with the truth of the situation and not run from it. These were the things that I had control over. After becoming aware of the facts, my decision was that lying, cheating, and stealing just to stay in business was not a good option. Besides, deception and lying were driving me deeper into depression, denial, and a loss of self-respect.

I decided to be more of a director and start thriving even in a difficult situation. As the creditors called, I began taking the calls and speaking with the creditors myself. No more deception and using my employees to screen the phone calls just to avoid an uncomfortable conversation. No longer did I want to have my employees tell our customers or employees that I wasn't in the office when in fact I was at my desk. I would take the call and deal with the issues. I simply stated the facts about what happened and explained what I could and couldn't do. This gave me some control and direction. I also felt better about myself. During this time, I started to investigate my financial options, list things that I needed to do, and take action. One action I decided to take was to meet in person with the owner of a bank that held one of my business loans.

I owed a lot of money to a bank just north of Denton, Texas. They had given me several loans and a significant credit line based on my business plan. However, my business was in default and doing poorly. I discovered that the bank owner lived several hours away, so I decided it was best to make a face-to-face visit instead of a phone conversation. As I drove to the bank, I imagined what the conversation would be like. I owed them thousands of dollars and couldn't pay it back. I did feel sad about the whole experience, and I wished the situation was different. However, I didn't have control over the sluggish economy or the fact that some of my commercial clients had filed for bankruptcy and didn't pay me. I did have control of my response to the situation. As bad as it was, I did have things I could do.

When I arrived at the bank, I was informed that the CEO of the bank wasn't in but would be back in a few hours. I waited for two and a half hours before he could see me. I remember watching him through the glass window as I waited. The CEO looked to be about seventy-five years old, and it appeared that this was going to be a difficult conversation because of the manner in which he was talking to a loan officer. He was very firm, decisive, and direct. My hands were sweating. I wanted to bolt out the door and avoid the meeting altogether. When I walked into his office, I sat down in a large leather chair and shared my story with him. I just started with the facts and shared with him my situation.

At the end of my story I said, "Listen, I owe you a lot of money. I don't have a clue how I'm going to pay you back. I just want to tell you I'm sorry. If you'll work with me, I'll do everything I can to make sure I take care of this. But you are going to have to work with me on restructuring these loans as well as kick in some more money for me to work things out."

The bank CEO said, "The whole banking institution is going through a current meltdown. The scandal with the savings and loan companies as well as dishonesty in the building industry has impacted this business as well as many others. We have hundreds of loans currently in default. Business is not good. Today the FBI is here doing an investigation on some of our loan officers. They claim some of my loan officers are taking kickbacks and bribes and passing off bad loans as good ones. However, thank you for taking the time to see us. Very few people have taken the time to meet with me or even call about their loans. Fewer still have called to apologize and try to work out a plan. So, this bank appreciates the time you took to drop by. I am sorry you had to wait so long."

Afterward, the CEO walked me to the door and again said he appreciated the time I took to share with him my situation. He gave me a warm handshake, and I felt he was sincere as he wished me good luck. In the end, the bank couldn't extend any more credit to me. Even so, I believe that my visit was time well spent. On the drive back home, I still didn't have a good solution for how things were going to work out for my business, but I felt very good that I had done the right thing.

As time went on, the market continued to slow down, and my business didn't pick back up. I wish I could tell you a happy ending. However, I was in my early thirties and over a million dollars in debt. After a long struggle, I finally closed the doors. The creditors came after me like starving barracudas. They were rude and ruthless. I tried to work with the ones I could, but eventually several forced the company into bankruptcy. Yet my largest creditor, the bank and its owner, never filed a claim of any kind. They never took action or hounded me in any way. I'm not sure why, but I think it had something to do with my face-to-face visit with the CEO. I think he understood that sometimes business deals don't work out, and he appreciated that I took responsibility for mine.

Taking responsibility and ownership in your situation is the essence of being a Thriver and a director. It's about taking credit for the things we do right and owning up to the things that don't go right, rather than shifting ownership elsewhere. When we are directors, we deal with our lives scene by scene—while never losing the vision of what we want the total picture to look like. Thrivers behave as directors when they:

- **Take the script and make it better.** Instead of wishing for a different "life script," they take the one that's given to them and improve it as they go.

- **Listen to their heart as well as outside advice.** Directors need propeller friends, as I explained in Chapter 4. And it's OK to listen to their advice, but remember that many times friends' suggestions are made with a skewed view of the situation. Seek the counsel of others, but listen to your instincts, too.

  Most often, when looking for direction, we have an internal voice that we listen to as well as external voices (e.g., friends, parents, teachers, church workers, consultants, experts, etc.) It is wise to decide what it is that you want to do, as well as seek wise counsel of others. However, if you don't know or don't have clarity on what you want to do, then you will end up where others suggest you go. I remember a friend of mine who wanted to be a dance instructor and eventually have her own dance studio. However, while working for a company as a teenager, the boss told her that becoming a dance instructor was a bad idea. Listening to that advice cost her the desire of her heart. That may have been good advice from her boss's perspective, but my friend lost sight of her vision because she wasn't listening to the longing in her inner voice.

- **Don't wait around for someone to bring them success.** Directors don't wait for success. They create it. Some people feel that others are luckier than they are. Directors understand that most "luck" is actually due to persistence and endurance. Their success comes through hard work and diligence. They are not waiting around for success to find them.

- **Are the boss when on the set.** Directors understand that they have ownership over their decisions, attitudes, and actions. They are their own boss, and they are accountable for what they create. There is a distinct difference when you meet an actor and then meet the director of a play. You know the director is in charge by the way he or she takes control of a situation. Directors let people know that they have a vision and a direction. Focusing on how and why I got in so much trouble in my first business didn't help me feel confident. As long as I was focusing on the past, I felt that I didn't have any control over it. However, focusing on the future and how better things would get, breaking down the debt into amounts I could pay, and then talking with the creditors about what I could do gave me a renewed hope and confidence.

- **Deal with the critics.** Critics are everywhere. Try doing something great, and soon you'll find a heckler in the crowd. Actors are devastated when the critics attack them; directors understand that not everyone will agree with their approach, yet they have a strong sense of self with the ability to stay focused on their goal.

- **Have a vision of what they want their life to look like.** Directors have a vision for the life they want. If you asked them about it, they will have a clear direction and purpose. They tend to be goal-oriented and work hard to achieve these goals despite the challenges. Their picture of their goals keeps them focused and keeps them going.

Summary

It's not bad to be an actor when you are surviving a crisis. However, if you want to transition into a more thriving life, at some point you are going to have to become a director in your own life play. Are you the one calling out, "Action!"? Do you have a vision of a life movie or play you want to write? Are you leading yourself to a better life and fulfilling your life goals? To become a Thriver, you will find yourself thinking about how *it can be done* and avoid thinking about how *it can't be done*. Planning and setting goals becomes very important, as well as developing clarity on your strengths and weaknesses. Review the following characteristics and see which ones best describe you and your approach to life right now. Share these with a friend who can tell you what characteristics he or she sees in you.

<u>*Surviving*</u>		<u>*Thriving*</u>
Actor	**vs.**	**Director**
- Can't be done		- Can be done
- Present-focused		- Future-focused
- Unclear identity		- Clear identity

In the next chapter, you will read about an ordinary person who went from surviving to thriving in an extraordinary way. Just as I used the surviving/thriving model to get through my divorce and other life experiences, my colleague Suzi has used it to keep her marriage together—and create an even stronger bond.

Insight

Actor Versus Director

Ask yourself these questions to see if you are an actor or director:

- Am I confident about my opinions, visions, and dreams, or am I acting out someone else's plan for me?
- Do I write my life script or just take the one I feel life hands me and respond?
- How am I taking my life script and making it better?
- How do I react to my critics?

Chapter Eight

Thriving in Action: Suzi's Story

After nearly two decades together, my husband Brad and I separated. It was the most devastating event of my life. Being a wife and a mother had been my most important calling. I had failed at the one thing I wanted the most. I felt empty, hopeless, scared, angry, and confused. I was sure my life was over. My first instinct was to hide, to pull the covers over my head and never wake up. Fortunately, my two sons gave me a reason to get out from under the covers and face the day. As Stepp and I wrote this book, I saw in myself all the behaviors of a Survivor. It wasn't until I made the conscious decision to thrive that the light came back and life became better.

At the start of the separation, I immediately went into self-preservation mode. The pain—deep, constant, and endless—put me in shock. I would not wish it upon my worst enemy. I didn't want to hurt, so I numbed myself. In a meeting or a group gathering, I often felt as though my body was present, but my mind and spirit were gone. All of my focus was on the pain. It's like when you have a toothache and all you can think of is how bad your tooth hurts. I lost my appetite, I couldn't sleep, and I cried more than I thought possible.

I remember looking in the mirror one morning after crying all night. It looked like I'd been beaten up. I had two black eyes from crying so hard! I didn't want to see or talk to anyone. I was a turtle who had pulled as far into my shell as I could. People told me later that they would see me and think that I had either developed an eating disorder or was seriously ill.

I read every book I could get my hands on, trying to figure out what I needed to do to "fix Brad" and how I could save my marriage. I have to admit my major focus was on what was wrong with *him*.

One close friend was my confidant. She was a huge blessing in my life. She kept me sane. I spent a lot of time telling and rehashing the story with her. I was definitely playing the victim. I remember telling her once that I didn't understand how so many other women we knew could treat their husbands so badly, but their husbands didn't leave them. Why did it happen to me? I had tried so hard; why was I being punished? I didn't deserve it.

I remember days when I didn't think I would get through. I'd call her, and she would listen to me for hours. I now see that I was a parasite. She was always patient, loving, and kind. I learned so much from her about how to treat others. She taught me about giving and truly putting another person's needs before my own. She would listen and sympathize, but she would never criticize Brad or put him down. Often she would even defend him and try to help me see his side. I often found this very irritating, but I realize now how wise she was.

Surviving Is Instinct. Thriving Is a Conscious Decision.

The actor phase was the easiest for me to move through. I much preferred being a parasite and victim who was just trying to survive the horror of facing a divorce. I never was big on doing what other people told me to do just because they thought it was best. As people found out we were separated, they were very free with their advice. I was surprised at much of what they said, considering that they really didn't know my circumstances, and I wasn't about to share it with them. The overwhelming advice I got was that I needed to be happy, that I just needed to hurry up, get the divorce, and find someone else.

Many books that I read and many people that I listened to were emphatic that I should worry only about me and my happiness. I have found out during this life lesson that to be a good wife, parent, and friend, the exact opposite is true. You have to ask, "What do I need to do for the other person?" Wouldn't you know it, that's when you really find happiness for yourself! I questioned whether or not people really had my best interests at heart. Many didn't. I learned who my real friends and supporters were. This caused some more pain, but also many blessings.

My faith, which was something I had taken for granted, deepened and strengthened unbelievably during this time. I had always had a core set of values that were never really tested, and one of them was that marriage was until death. I felt strongly that God wanted me to stay and fight for my marriage and to honor my vows. Every time I was ready to heed the advice of others and go ahead with the divorce, I would talk with God. I had no doubt that He didn't want me to give up, that His will was for this marriage to survive. Many times I would scream at God, "Enough! You can't think this will ever heal. Why are you punishing me? I can't do this." His message never changed. Finally, in defeat, I started my day with the prayer: "Show me your will and give me the strength to live it."

During this time I heard a couple on TV tell the story of their separation and how their faith in God brought them back together after five years! I remember thinking I could never last that long! As the old saying goes, never say never!

Finally, the Decision to Move beyond Surviving to Thriving

I can't say exactly when I quit surviving and decided to thrive. It was longer than it should have been. Several things finally seemed to make sense at once. The first was that I still had a lot of life ahead of me, and I couldn't wait around for someone else to take control of it and make it better. I decided to quit worrying about what was wrong with Brad and worry about what was wrong with me. As my focus shifted, I began to show the first signs of self-growth. What role had I played? What should I have done differently? What did I do to cause the breakdown of our marriage? These were hard questions—and, when I got honest with myself, very painful answers.

One of the many books that found its way into my hands was *The Power of a Praying Wife* by Stormie Omartian.[1] To this day, I still say one of the prayers from that book every morning. In the book, the first step in praying for your husband is to ask God to change you. Nothing would heal or get better until I was willing to admit my shortcomings and take responsibility for the problem. It was very difficult to shift the focus to my own shortcomings. It was hard to admit I was stubborn, selfish, whiney, needy, and sometimes cruel. Once I did it, though, a wonderful thing happened. I became the warrior and regained control of my life. Finally, there was something I could do—there were productive steps I could take! I could work on *my* weaknesses. I had a new goal: to "fix" me! The prayer "Change me, God" became a mantra for me.

A wise person told me that while none of us knew if Brad and I would reconcile or divorce, I would have to live with myself no matter what happened. So why didn't I use this time to become a stronger, better person? My focus shifted. I quit crying and feeding on friends' sympathies and stepped up to the plate as a player. It wasn't easy; sometimes it was downright terrifying, and I wanted to go back to being the turtle in my protective shell. I kept remembering that no matter what happened, life would be better if I were stronger. I knew I wasn't alone; God was always there giving me strength, peace, and courage in the midst of my fears and doubts. Good friends and family were there, too.

It continues to amaze me that when we change ourselves, others change the way they respond to us. Moving into director mode, I began to take responsibility for my part in the breakdown of our marriage, and there was a lot to take responsibility for. Brad started responding to me differently. I started seeing the positive things he was doing and stopped focusing on the negative things. I began seeing a man of character who was also struggling and trying to do what was right. My perception of him changed when I changed my behavior.

We were down to the final steps in the divorce process; all that was left was to sign the papers. It was near the end of the calendar year, and if we were divorced by year's end, there would be a significant tax advantage financially for us. We didn't sign, and I will never forget Brad's response when I reminded him that we would lose a lot of money if we didn't get it done. He said, "It doesn't matter." We began a slow and cautious reconciliation. In 2005, we celebrated our twenty-fifth wedding anniversary. As I said earlier, I wouldn't wish the pain of this experience on anyone, but because of what we went through, we are better as a couple, we are better parents to our sons, and we are closer to God.

We don't get to coast down the hill and live happily ever after. We have to work at it and fight for our marriage every day. The focus has to be, "What can I do to serve my spouse?" and not, "What do I want?" We have to live as Thrivers, and it isn't always easy. One thing is for certain, though: we would have never gotten *here* without traveling *there*.

Thriving Is a Learned Behavior

Suzi's story emphasizes that thriving is a learned behavior. How do you learn it? Practice, practice, practice! Here are seven signs that you've moved from surviving to thriving.

1. *Thankfulness*—**You are grateful for your life and believe there's a point in it all.** Even though you've faced the darkness, you can still embrace the light.

2. *Humor*—**You're laughing.** Humor is a powerful tool. It turns us around and keeps things in balance when life seems unfair. It's also an easy way to strengthen the heart muscle. Twenty seconds of laughter can equal three minutes of strenuous exercise.

3. *Release*—**You can let go of the past.** You have your feelings, but you don't let your feelings have you. You let go of bad things when they are over and argue effectively against your self-defeating thoughts.

4. *Influence*—**You respond appropriately when the heat is on.** Remember the carrots, eggs, and coffee beans illustration from Chapter Three? Rather than wilting in the face of adversity or hardening your heart, you release a part of yourself to influence your situation, touching others with your richness of spirit.

5. *Vision*—**You can envision the possible.** You use your imagination to enhance the quality of your life in the here and now. You dream big and invest your time and energy into creating a way to make your goals come true. It's the

age-old question, "Is the glass half full, or is it half empty?" Half-empty glasses bring half-empty results, while a positive outlook can fill up the world with new possibilities.

6. ***Encouragement*—You surround yourself with a supportive team.** You realize you can't go it alone and have invited people into your life who will love and support you at every turn. Be sure you have "propellers"—the people who can help you move forward and focus on your options. Be part of a support team for others, too. Let others know you are there to help them get to the top of the mountain. You will grow through the experience and create lifelong friends.

7. ***Responsibility*—You're making things happen.** Rather than lamenting your plight, you're putting one foot in front of the other and getting on with your life. You've turned adversity to your advantage with a more aware, appreciative, and ardent involvement in the activities of daily life.

Continuing the Process

By reading this book, you have taken the first steps toward a more thriving life. Congratulations! To continue developing a thriving mentality, you'll want to start applying what you have learned right away. The first step is to review what you have learned about the following four categories for Surviving versus Thriving behaviors. Then, determine which characteristics best describe where you are in various areas in your life. If you're not sure, then consider spending time with a trusted friend to get honest feedback on these areas. Following the principles you've learned in this book, begin to make the changes you need to make to become a Thriver instead of merely a Survivor.

I would encourage you to spend time and think about the areas in life that most frustrate you, and then write them down. Think about the past and the experiences you have been through, good or bad. Think about what you learned about your past and how you are using this information to move forward (or remain stuck). Stop complaining about what you hate and how you can't do anything about it and begin to ask yourself how you can make the changes needed to thrive and create the life you want.

	Surviving		_Thriving_
1.	**Self-Preservation**	**vs.**	**Self-Growth**
	- Shocked		- Healing
	- Withdrawn		- Engaged
	- Helpless		- Empowered
2.	**Victim**	**vs.**	**Warrior**
	- Blaming		- Accountable
	- Hopeless		- Determined
	- Emotional		- Logical
3.	**Parasite**	**vs.**	**Player**
	- Passive		- Assertive
	- Energy-absorbing		- Energy-producing
	- Reactive		- Proactive
4.	**Actor**	**vs.**	**Director**
	- Can't be done		- Can be done
	- Present-focused		- Future-focused
	- Unclear identity		- Clear identity

Seeing a Greater Purpose

One recent evening while thinking about my life journey, I was sitting on my back patio, looking up at the sky and the hugeness of the heavens. The sky was clear and the stars were more brilliant than I have seen them in a while. Their luminosity brought a quiet stirring from deep within. I felt a joy and a thankfulness that I was able write this book to help others. I was thankful for my team at work who helps to fulfill my vision. And thankful for the love of my children and how much joy I get from them. It made me so thankful for all that has happened to me—the financial failure, relationship failure, the job losses, loss of friends and family, the struggles and challenges that continue to come.

Just sitting there that night, it felt like a whisper from a higher power—a reminder that someone greater made the stars, the heavens, and all that we see. That there is an order to things, and that I wasn't a mistake or an accident. It was an interesting thought that maybe there is a greater purpose for our struggles than what we see. Maybe there is a purpose for your struggles and a reason for you reading this book.

While I was contemplating these things, at that moment a shooting star with a long tail rocketed across the darkness! I was reminded again that whatever the turbulence of this life, there is a reason to thrive. However, it was late, and I needed to get to bed for an early morning meeting. As I started to head inside, I picked up my cell phone from the patio table and funny thing... it was covered in star dust.

Epilogue

Life is hard, and I find that making changes isn't easy. There isn't a fix-it pill that you can take so that when you wake up in the morning, the world you want magically appears. However, you can make a decision to move forward and use your life experiences to create a better life for yourself and others.

There are a lot of stories about people who have endured incredible hardship and disappointments. Maybe you haven't yet experienced a life-changing event. Maybe it's just been a series of little disappointments or an unsettling feeling that there could be more in life for you. I would encourage you to consider *why* you might be just surviving this life and discover what it will take to get you to your next level.

I have realized that life is more about how I handle adversity than the adversity itself. My ability to handle stress comes from my awareness to see how I am acting at the moment as well as the things that cause stress.

Sometimes I felt like the only nail that is sticking out of a piece of wood. I'm exposed and vulnerable and then "WHAM!" a hammer comes down and knocks me back into place. For instance, I would often work hard to save some money, placing a little back in an account in case of a rainy day. Only to find that something happens, circumstances change, and there goes the savings. I just could not seem to get ahead in life. I didn't like living from paycheck to paycheck, but that had been the story of my life. I felt stuck, just surviving the next financial crisis.

Then I chose a more thriving mentality. I started reading books on how to handle money and rethink how I was spending it. I talked to people who seemed to be better at money management than me and discovered what they were doing differently. Having found a successful approach has changed my behavior. Today I am in much better financial shape. And as I learn and grow more, I feel better about my direction. I was tired of being the nail and decided to be a hammer.

How do you know if you are in a thriving mode? You will find that even in your struggles you have a renewed hope and excitement about life. There is freshness to your day, like the feeling of a cool morning right after a long, hot summer. It's kind of like being in a desert and coming across an oasis with fresh water. Yes, you're tired, worn out, and hurting, but the new hope that a better life is right around the corner reenergizes your soul. You're going beyond surviving to thriving.

I want to emphasize that it all has to start with you. If you desire a more thriving life, then you have to make the first step. Consider this book an ongoing invitation to live, to laugh, to do good things, to love, and to be loved.

Coming Soon!

Survive or Thrive? Seminar

Survive or Thrive?

The seminar covers material in this book and more:

- Moving beyond just surviving
- Recognize you may be stuck in survivor mode
- Facing adversity and handling change
- Discover strategies that enable positive change
- How to avoid becoming a victim
- How to take charge of your future
- Understand what habits keep you from thriving
- Gain skills to create the life you want
- Apply the concepts to change your circumstances

For more information on how you can launch into a more thriving life, please contact us at:

TurnAround Solutions, LLC
Marketing Department
P.O. Box 10111
Tyler, TX 75711
903-533-0591
E-mail: getthecure@turnaroundsolutions.net
Website: www.turnaroundsolutions.net

IMPROVING SALES, LEADERSHIP, AND RELATIONSHIP SKILLS

Got a good surviving-to-thriving story? Please e-mail it to us at getthecure@turnaroundsolutions.net. We would love to see how this book has helped shape the events of your life.

Other Training from TurnAround Solutions

Team Building

Communication

Conflict Resolution

Coaching Style Leadership

Effectively Manage and Supervise Your Team

Create Opportunity for Selling, Prospecting, and Networking

Managing Salespeople

Corporate Culture

Customer Service

Hiring and Employee Development Assessment Tools

Endnotes

Chapter 1: No One Said Life Is Fair

[1]Berit Kjos, *A Wardrobe from the King* (Wheaton, IL: Victor Books, 1988) 45-46, www.crossroad.to.

Chapter 2: Learning to Manage Our Self-Talk

[1]One of the best resources on this topic of managing the things you tell yourself is a book entitled *Crucial Conversations, Tools for Talking When Stakes Are High*, McGraw-Hill Publisher, authors Kerry Patterson, Joseph Grenny, Ron McMillan, and Al Switzler.

Chapter 8: Thriving in Action: Suzi's Story

[1]Stormie Omartian, *The Power of a Praying Wife* (Eugene: Harvest House Publishers, 1997).

About the Authors

Stepp Stevens Sydnor

Stepp has twenty-eight years of experience in working with startup and established organizations to help improve their business processes, employee morale, and sales revenues. He is also a lifelong student of human behavior from both the psychological and spiritual perspective. The synergy between his business experience and his understanding of human behavior has brought a uniquely integrated perspective to his business and his coaching.

In 1999, Stepp founded The TurnAround Group, now TurnAround Solutions, LLC, to help companies improve their profitability by focusing on their employees. He has developed training, coaching, and mentoring programs in the areas of sales, leadership, culture, personal development, and stress management. Clients have ranged from public-sector organizations such as PricewaterhouseCoopers and Dallas Housing Authority to industry leaders such as Cox Communications, Sam's Club, and Robroy Industries.

An accomplished speaker, Stepp conducts seminars regularly for corporations and other organizations. He is the father of three teenagers and lives in East Texas.

Suzi Streit

Suzi is a trainer, coach, and motivational speaker with TurnAround Solutions. She works with TurnAround Solutions CEO Stepp Stevens Sydnor to deliver dynamic leadership, communication, and team-building programs to the business community. She also provides one-on-one training that ensures tools learned in training become life habits.

Before joining TurnAround Solutions, Suzi worked for ten years as a certified instructor with the Dale Carnegie Program. Her skills in human dynamics have been the foundation of her work with TurnAround Solutions. She teaches a wide range of courses designed to improve leadership skills and enhance professional and personal interactions—from *Crucial Conversations*® by VitalSmarts™, for which she is a certified instructor, to DiSC Style Analysis™. Suzi has also developed several of TurnAround Solutions' innovative, interactive training curriculums, from time management to coaching style management.

Suzi has a degree in business administration from Stephen F. Austin State University. She and her husband, Brad, are the parents of two sons.

978-0-595-42294-4
0-595-42294-2

Printed in the United States
204253BV00002B/331-417/P